STECK-VAUGHN
SUPERSTARS
IN ACTION
COURAGE & DARING

Randal C. Hill

Steck-Vaughn Company

A Subsidiary of National Education Corporation

ABOUT THE AUTHOR

Randal C. Hill teaches English, reading, and history of rock music at Fairvalley High School in Covina, California. A former disc jockey and writer of children's stories, he earned his M.A. in Education from California State Polytechnic University in Pomona, where he received the Distinguished Alumnus Award in 1981.

The Superstars in Action Series

Superstars in Action
Courage and Daring

Superstars in Action
Auto Racing

Acknowledgments

Executive Editor
Leslie Ford

Project Editor
Diane Sharpe

Designers
Bonnie Baumann
Sharon Golden

ISBN 0-8114-1598-8

Copyright © 1989 Steck-Vaughn Company.
All rights reserved. No part of the material protected by this copyright may be reproduced or utilized in any form or by any means, electronic or mechanical, including photocopying, recording, or by any information storage and retrieval system, without permission in writing from the copyright owner.
Requests for permission to make copies of any part of the work should be mailed to: Copyright Permissions, Steck-Vaughn Company, P.O. Box 26015, Austin, TX 78755.
Printed in the United States of America.

3 4 5 6 7 8 9 0 VP 92 91 90

Dear Reader,

This is a book about people like you and me. Most of them have led ordinary lives. But one day, each of them decided to do something extraordinary.

The people in this book had different reasons for making that decision. Some wanted to do something no one had ever done before. Some wanted to show how much people with disabilities could accomplish. Others simply craved adventure.

These men and women followed many different dreams. But all of them dared to risk their lives to reach a goal. And each of them had the courage to believe in his or her abilities.

Since most of these people didn't expect to become famous, they were surprised by the attention they received. After all, they were just ordinary people doing what they wanted to do. But it seems to me that they also did something very important for us. By reading their stories, we learn that we can reach goals which often seem impossible. Furthermore, the stories make us realize that there really *aren't* ordinary people in this world. There is something unique and special about each and every one of us.

Randal C. Hill

CONTENTS

Voyager's Victory   2

The Fastest Woman on Earth   10

The Flight of Double Eagle II   18

Breaking the Sound Barrier   26

Grandma Fuji   34

The Impossible Swim   42

Man in Motion   **50**

On Top of the World   **58**

The Voyage of *Outward Leg*   **66**

A Long Walk   **74**

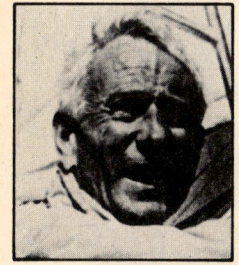

Alone with the Sea   **82**

On Two Wheels   **90**

Glossary   **98**
Answer Key   **103**

Voyager's Victory

Voyager is about to take off. But something is wrong. It's so loaded down with fuel that the wings drag the ground. If it doesn't take off before the runway ends, it will crash. The fuel it is carrying will burst into flames! At the last moment, the plane lifts off. For Dick Rutan and Jeana Yeager, it's a rough beginning. But things will get even worse before they get back home.

A Handmade Plane

Dick Rutan and Jeana Yeager met at an air show in 1980. Dick had been a fighter pilot in the Vietnam War. Jeana flew for fun. She had set nine speed and **endurance** records. Dick and Jeana were thinking about starting an airplane sales business. They wanted to find a way to attract attention to themselves and their business.

One day Dick and Jeana told Dick's brother Burt about their plans. Burt, an airplane designer, told them he could design a lightweight airplane that could carry enough fuel to go around the world. Dick and Jeana could be the first pilots to fly around the world without stopping or **refueling**.

Dick and Jeana knew it would be a dangerous flight. But they were willing to take the risk. They rented a shed at the Mojave airport. For five years, Dick and Jeana **invested** most of their time and money in the **experimental** plane. They named it Voyager. It was built by hand out of special lightweight materials.

Close Quarters

Finally Voyager was ready to fly. Most of the plane was hollow for fuel storage. This made it very dangerous to fly. Even a small spark could cause it to explode. Its wings were very long and **flexible**. The slightest air **turbulence** made flying Voyager like being in a rowboat in rough seas.

Voyager was not built for comfort. The **cockpit** was only 3½ feet wide by 7½ feet long. Dick says it looked like a telephone booth on its side. It had only one seat for the pilot. The passenger had to lie on the floor. Dick and Jeana took turns flying the plane.

Since the cockpit was so small, there was no space to cook. Dick and Jeana had to eat prepared foods. They didn't even have room to change into clean clothes. Every time the plane was bounced around by the wind, they were bruised. The noise from the engines was so loud that Dick and Jeana had to wear earphones to keep from damaging their hearing.

A Place in History

During their flight, Dick and Jeana faced one emergency after another. On the second day of the flight, they had to fly around a **typhoon** with 75-mile-per-hour winds. But they couldn't fly too far off course or they might fly over Vietnam. Vietnam is a country that is not friendly toward the U.S. Dick and Jeana were afraid that they might be shot down.

The worst part of the trip came at the end. Dick and Jeana had to fly through another storm. Suddenly, both of Voyager's engines stopped! The plane began falling toward the Pacific Ocean. Dick finally got the engines started. It was a very close call.

Voyager landed at Edwards Air Force Base nine days after it took off. The flight pushed Dick and Jeana's flying skills to the limit. It tested their will to **survive**. Dick and Jeana had earned a place in **aviation** history. President Reagan awarded them the Presidential Citizens Medal. And Voyager was sent to the National Air and Space Museum in Washington, D.C., where it will always have a place of honor.

Remembering Facts

In the blank, write the letter of the best ending for each sentence.

_____ 1. Dick Rutan and Jeana Yeager met
a. in Vietnam.   b. at an airshow.   c. in a restaurant.

_____ 2. In the Vietnam War, Dick had been a
a. fighter pilot.   b. reporter.   c. paratrooper.

_____ 3. Building Voyager took
a. five months.   b. three years.   c. five years.

_____ 4. Most of Voyager was hollow so that Jeana and Dick could store
a. fuel.   b. food.   c. clean clothes.

_____ 5. Voyager has
a. two seats.   b. one seat.   c. no seats.

_____ 6. The worst part of the trip came when
a. the engines stopped.   b. Jeana was bruised.
c. they ran out of food.

_____ 7. The Voyager trip took
a. four days.   b. six days.   c. nine days.

_____ 8. Voyager is now in the
a. Wax Museum.   b. National Air and Space Museum.
c. President's back yard.

Finding the Sequence

Write **1** before the sentence that tells what happened first in the story. Write **2** before the sentence that tells what happened next, and so on.

_____ Voyager landed at Edwards Air Force Base.

_____ Dick and Jeana rented a shed at the Mojave Airport.

_____ Dick and Jeana had to fly around a typhoon.

_____ Dick Rutan and Jeana Yeager met.

_____ Voyager was ready to fly.

Using Context

Write the correct word in each blank. Choose from the words below. Use each word only once.

<table>
<tr><td>Jeana</td><td>never</td><td>around</td><td>handmade</td></tr>
<tr><td>did</td><td>designed</td><td>survive</td><td>dangerous</td></tr>
</table>

Dick Rutan and Jeana Yeager _____1_____ something that had _____2_____ been done before. They flew _____3_____ the world without stopping to refuel. They did it in a _____4_____ plane that was _____5_____ by Dick's brother. The nine-day trip was _____6_____. Dick and _____7_____ could have died. But their will to _____8_____ brought them back home.

Drawing Conclusions

Finish each sentence by writing the best answer.

1. Voyager was very dangerous to fly because _____

2. Dick and Jeana had to eat prepared foods because _____

3. Dick and Jeana had to wear earphones because _____

4. Dick and Jeana didn't want to fly over Vietnam because _____

Identifying Facts and Opinions

A fact is something that can be proven true. An opinion is what someone thinks about something. Write **F** before each statement that is a fact. Write **O** before each statement that is an opinion.

    _____ 1. Flying around the world without stopping to refuel is crazy!

    _____ 2. Voyager's cockpit was 3½ feet wide by 7½ feet long.

    _____ 3. The noise from Voyager's engines was very loud.

    _____ 4. Burt Rutan is the best airplane designer in the world.

    _____ 5. Dick and Jeana met in 1980.

    _____ 6. Dick and Jeana shouldn't have taken the risk they took.

    _____ 7. Dick was a fighter pilot in the Vietnam War.

    _____ 8. Voyager was built by hand.

    _____ 9. Dick and Jeana's flying skills are without equal.

    _____ 10. Voyager is now in a museum.

Writing Your Ideas

Imagine a telephone booth on its side. Picture yourself lying inside it for nine days. Write two sentences about the way you feel on the first day. Write two sentences about the way you feel on the ninth day.

First Day _____

_____

Ninth Day _____

_____

Using Vocabulary

Use each of the following words in a sentence. Show by your sentence that you understand the meaning of the word. If you need help, use the Glossary.

1. cockpit _____
   _____

2. refuel _____
   _____

3. typhoon _____
   _____

4. endurance _____
   _____

5. survive _____
   _____

6. invest _____
   _____

7. aviation _____
   _____

8. flexible _____
   _____

9. turbulence _____
   _____

10. experimental _____
    _____

The Fastest Woman on Earth

🌎 To the people watching that December day, the race car looked like a jet plane without wings. The roar of the 48,000-**horsepower** engine thundered across the dry lake bed. But the car's driver never heard a sound. Kitty O'Neil, the fastest woman on Earth, is deaf.

A Silent World

Kitty O'Neil was just four months old when she got the measles, mumps, and chicken pox all at once. Because of high fever, Kitty lost her hearing.

Kitty's mother wanted her to live a normal life. She went to college to learn how to teach the deaf. "She taught me to swim and to **respond** to questions when I was a baby," Kitty remembers. "Then she taught me how to read lips and speak."

Kitty went to school for the first time in the third grade. She was a good student. Kitty's mother suggested she take piano lessons. She could tell which notes she was playing by feeling the **vibrations** of the sounds. Kitty learned to play both the piano and the cello!

Taking the Plunge

When she was 12, Kitty started swimming **competitively**. She also wanted to dive. But her **instructors** didn't think she could do it. They thought being deaf would affect her sense of balance. At a swim meet in Oklahoma, Kitty got a chance to prove them wrong. "One of our team's divers didn't show up," she remembers. "On **impulse** I asked the coach to let me try." Kitty won first place! She went on to become an excellent diver. Before she quit the sport, she had won 38 blue ribbons, 17 first-place trophies, and 31 gold medals.

After diving, Kitty tried other sports. She raced cars and boats. She did skydiving and **scuba** diving. Kitty even set a women's **water-skiing** speed record in 1970. She was pulled behind a boat going nearly 105 miles per hour! "I guess I like danger and thrills," says Kitty. "But mostly I want always to have a goal, some dream I can try for."

In 1971, Kitty met Duffy Hambleton at a motorcycle meet. She had started racing motorcycles cross-country. Unlike other racers, she couldn't hear what gear the motorcycle was in. And she had no way of knowing a competitor was coming up behind her. "She was unbelievable," Duffy says. "I couldn't

Kitty O'Neil performs a dangerous stunt in a van.

imagine being able to ride a motorcycle the way she could." Duffy and Kitty were married within a year.

A New World Record

Kitty thought her husband's job as a stunt man looked exciting. "Teach me how to do stunts," she asked him. Although almost all stunt people were men, Duffy agreed. Kitty was a **natural**.

For the next two years, Kitty practiced falling, faking fights, and rolling cars. Soon Kitty was one of the most popular stunt women in Hollywood. She was one of the first two women elected to Stunts Unlimited, an important stunt men's **organization**.

Kitty has done one stunt which has never been attempted by another woman. She did a car rollover in which explosives are used to lift one side of the car!

Being a stunt woman was not enough for Kitty. She wanted to break the World Land Speed Record for women. In 1976, Kitty strapped herself into a 38-foot, rocket-powered vehicle. She hit the **accelerator** and tore off at 512.7 miles per hour! It took her five miles to stop. Kitty O'Neil had become the fastest woman on Earth.

"I can do anything," Kitty once said. "I like to do things people say I can't do because I'm deaf. I have to work harder than some. But look at the fun I have proving they're wrong."

Remembering Facts

Read each sentence below. Write **T** if the sentence is true. Write **F** if the sentence is false.

_____ 1. Kitty lost her hearing when she was four years old.

_____ 2. Kitty's mother went to college to learn how to teach the deaf.

_____ 3. Kitty went to school for the first time in the first grade.

_____ 4. Kitty was never able to play the piano.

_____ 5. Kitty started swimming competitively when she was 12.

_____ 6. Kitty doesn't like to do dangerous things.

_____ 7. Kitty met her husband at a swim meet.

_____ 8. Duffy taught Kitty how to do stunts.

_____ 9. Kitty was one of the first two women elected to Stunts Unlimited.

_____ 10. Kitty O'Neil is the fastest woman on Earth.

Finding the Sequence

Write **1** before the sentence that tells what happened first in the story. Write **2** before the sentence that tells what happened next, and so on.

_____ Kitty became a diver.

_____ Kitty and Duffy got married.

_____ Kitty lost her hearing.

_____ Kitty became a stunt woman.

_____ Kitty started swimming competitively.

Using Context

Write the correct word in each blank. Choose from the words below. Use each word only once.

    anything   them   harder   four
    normal   tell   lost   her

Kitty O'Neil was _____(1)_____ months old when she _____(2)_____ her hearing. But this didn't keep _____(3)_____ from living a _____(4)_____ life. People used to _____(5)_____ Kitty there were things she couldn't do because she was deaf. But she proved _____(6)_____ wrong! Kitty says she can do _____(7)_____. She just has to work _____(8)_____ than some people.

Drawing Conclusions

Finish each sentence by writing the best answer.

1. Kitty O'Neil lost her hearing because _____

2. Kitty's swimming instructors didn't think she could dive because _____

3. When Duffy met Kitty he thought she was unbelievable because _____

4. Kitty O'Neil is called the fastest woman on Earth because _____

Identifying Facts and Opinions

Write **F** before each statement that is a fact. Write **O** before each statement that is an opinion.

_____ 1. Kitty's mother taught her how to read lips and speak.

_____ 2. Women shouldn't be allowed to do stunts.

_____ 3. Kitty set a women's water-skiing speed record in 1970.

_____ 4. Kitty's mother is the most loving mother in the world.

_____ 5. Kitty plays the cello and the piano.

_____ 6. People shouldn't have told Kitty what she could or couldn't do.

_____ 7. Kitty broke the World Land Speed Record for women in 1976.

_____ 8. Kitty met her future husband at a motorcycle meet.

_____ 9. Kitty shouldn't take so many risks!

_____ 10. Kitty O'Neil is the bravest woman on Earth.

Writing Your Ideas

People kept telling Kitty there were many things she couldn't do because she was deaf. But she worked hard and proved them all wrong. Write about something you've done that other people didn't think you could do.

_____
_____
_____
_____
_____
_____

Using Vocabulary

Write the correct word in each sentence.

accelerator	impulse	respond
scuba	horsepower	natural
vibration	water-skiing	instructor
competitively		

1. A unit used to measure the power of an engine is called _____.

2. The pedal that controls the speed of a car is called the _____.

3. To answer is to _____.

4. When you do something suddenly and without much thought, you act on _____.

5. Equipment used for breathing while swimming underwater is called _____.

6. When you are born with the ability to do something well, you are a _____.

7. The sport of skiing on the water is called _____.

8. Another name for teacher is _____.

9. When you do something _____, your goal is to win.

10. A quivering or trembling motion is called a _____.

17

The Flight of Double Eagle II

🌐 In August, 1978, President Jimmy Carter sent a telegram to three Americans in Paris, France. It read, "Your daring voyage through the silent sky is a welcome reminder that **individual** acts of **bravery** and skill still capture our imagination." America was celebrating. The three men had become the first people to cross the Atlantic Ocean in a balloon.

The First Try

One day in 1977, businessman Max Anderson called his friend Ben Abruzzo. They were both **amateur balloonists**. "What would you think about you and me flying the Atlantic?" he asked. Fourteen attempts had been made to cross the Atlantic in a balloon. All had failed, and five people had been killed. "Let's do it," said Ben.

Max and Ben called their balloon "Double Eagle." It was named for Charles Lindbergh, whose nickname was "Lone Eagle." Lindbergh was the first man to fly an airplane non-stop across the Atlantic alone.

But Max and Ben were not as lucky as Lindbergh had been. Severe storms blew them off course. Ben got very sick and nearly died from **exposure**. The Double Eagle landed in the water off the coast of Iceland. A helicopter rescued Max and Ben. Still, they were determined to try again.

A Second Chance

Ben met Larry Newman when Larry landed his **hang glider** in Ben's front yard. He had taken off from a nearby mountain. Ben wanted to learn to hang glide. Larry taught him, and the two became friends. When it was time for Max and Ben to make their second attempt, Larry asked to come with them.

On August 11, 1978, the three lifted off from Presque Isle, Maine, in their new balloon, Double Eagle II. The black-and-silver balloon was 11 stories high. The red and yellow **gondola** was also a boat, so if the men had to land in the ocean, they could stay afloat. They had computers aboard to guide them and radios so they could keep in touch with their ground crew.

Max, Ben, and Larry struggled against storms and **downdrafts**. Once, it got so cold that ice formed on the balloon. The extra weight caused it to fall dangerously low. They threw enough **ballast** overboard to keep the balloon in the air.

"There are no books or music," says Max, "but there is the whole world to see. It's completely silent,

Max, Larry, and Ben (l. to r.) are tired but happy after their landing.

and you move with the clouds. The world going by underneath you is such a **magnificent** sight that you have to force yourself to sleep when it is time to do so."

Near the end of the journey, the winds died down. The men were afraid they would have to land in the sea. But the winds picked up again and carried them over Ireland and England. They wanted to land where Lindbergh had landed, at Le Bourget Airfield in France. As they drifted over the French coast, a group of small planes and helicopters flew by in salute.

The Eagle Has Landed

Nearly six days and 3,100 miles after liftoff, the three men landed in a barley field near Miserey, France. They were only 50 miles away from Le Bourget. Thousands of people were waiting to see them land. Max, Ben, and Larry were heroes!

Like Charles Lindbergh before them, Max, Ben, and Larry did something no one had done before. They were willing to risk their lives to challenge the limits of man's ability. "Unless frontiers are challenged from time to time," says Ben Abruzzo, "we won't move forward as a society."

Remembering Facts

In the blank, write the letter of the best ending for each sentence.

_____ 1. The Double Eagle was named for
 a. nobody in particular.   b. Charles Lindbergh.
 c. Ben's pet eagle.

_____ 2. The flight of the Double Eagle was
 a. a failure.   b. a success.   c. fun.

_____ 3. Ben and Larry met
 a. at an air show.   b. in Ben's front yard.   c. in college.

_____ 4. Double Eagle II was
 a. two stories high.   b. six stories high.   c. 11 stories high.

_____ 5. Double Eagle II lifted off from
 a. New York.   b. Paris.   c. Maine.

_____ 6. Near the end of the journey of Double Eagle II,
 a. the winds died down.   b. the three men were bored.
 c. Ben, Max, and Larry ran out of books to read.

_____ 7. The Double Eagle II flight lasted nearly
 a. six days.   b. six months.   c. 10 days.

_____ 8. Double Eagle II landed
 a. at Le Bourget.   b. in a barley field.   c. in Ireland.

Finding the Sequence

Write **1** before the sentence that tells what happened first in the story. Write **2** before the sentence that tells what happened next, and so on.

_____ A group of small planes flew by to salute Double Eagle II.

_____ Larry landed his hang glider in Ben's front yard.

_____ Double Eagle II landed in France.

_____ Ben and Max attempted to cross the Atlantic in the Double Eagle.

_____ Double Eagle II lifted off from Presque Isle.

Using Context

Write the correct word in each blank. Choose from the words below. Use each word only once.

    him   force   sight   at
    never   exciting   balloon   see

Flying in a _____ was an _____ experience
                   1   2
for Max Anderson. He was _____ bored. After all, he
                                       3
could _____ the whole world beneath _____.
             4   5
He says it was such a beautiful _____ that he had to
                                                  6
_____ himself to sleep _____ night.
    7   8

Drawing Conclusions

Finish each sentence by writing the best answer.

1. The flight of the Double Eagle failed because _____
_____
_____

2. If Double Eagle II had landed in the ocean, it would have stayed afloat because _____
_____

3. Max Anderson didn't miss having books or music on the balloon because _____
_____

4. One day, Double Eagle II fell dangerously low because _____
_____
_____

Identifying Facts and Opinions

Write F before each statement that is a fact. Write O before each statement that is an opinion.

_____ 1. There is nothing as exciting as flying in a balloon.

_____ 2. Double Eagle II landed in August, 1978.

_____ 3. It wasn't nice of Larry to land on Ben's front yard!

_____ 4. Larry taught Ben how to hang glide.

_____ 5. Charles Lindbergh's nickname was "Lone Eagle."

_____ 6. Double Eagle II had computers and radios aboard.

_____ 7. The people living on the French coast are friendlier than any other people.

_____ 8. The three men should have taken something to read on the balloon.

_____ 9. Miserey, France, is 50 miles away from Le Bourget.

_____ 10. Max, Ben, and Larry are the most daring men in the world.

Writing Your Ideas

Flying across the Atlantic Ocean in a balloon is very dangerous. Five people have been killed in the attempt. If you had the chance to try this, would you take the risk? Explain your answer.

Using Vocabulary

Use the clues to complete the puzzle. Choose from the words in the box.

individual
balloonist
hang glider
bravery
exposure
downdraft
gondola
magnificent
ballast
amateur

Across
3. downward movement of air
4. courage
5. beautiful or grand
7. a person who travels in a balloon
8. the condition of being exposed
9. a person who takes part in a sport for fun

Down
1. a kite-like device
2. having to do with one person
4. something heavy
6. where passengers ride in a balloon

25

Breaking the Sound Barrier

Chuck Yeager had two broken ribs. But he didn't want to delay the **mission**. He climbed into the cockpit and fired the engines. The needle on his **speedometer** went past the mark for **Mach 1**. Suddenly his flight became very smooth. Chuck had made history. He was doing what many experts thought was impossible. He was flying faster than the speed of sound!

Learning to Fly

Chuck Yeager grew up in Hamlin, West Virginia. The people who lived there didn't have much money. But they always managed to get by. Chuck spent his free time in the hills. He played, hunted, and fished with the other boys.

When Chuck was 15, he saw his first airplane. It had crashed in a cornfield near town. Chuck didn't know he was looking at his future.

After Chuck graduated from high school, an Army Air Corps **recruiter** came to town. Men were needed to serve in World War II. Chuck decided to sign up.

The world outside the West Virginia hills seemed strange to Chuck. Because he spoke with a heavy accent, people had trouble understanding him. But Chuck was good with machines, and he became an airplane mechanic. The first time Chuck rode in a plane, he got sick. He never wanted to fly again.

Chuck soon changed his mind about flying. He found out that he could get a higher **rank** if he signed up for pilot training. After the first few flights, Chuck began to love flying. He also enjoyed finding out everything he could about how his plane worked. Chuck became the best flier in his class. He was selected to become a fighter pilot.

On one of his first missions, Chuck was shot down over enemy territory. He parachuted down and hid from the Germans. Chuck managed to escape to Spain. Soon, he returned to **combat**. He flew many missions and became an **ace pilot**.

The X-1

After his combat duty was over, Chuck became a test pilot for the Air Force. Chuck's commander, Colonel Boyd, had a difficult decision to make. The Air Force planned to try to fly the X-1 airplane faster than the speed of sound! Colonel Boyd had to choose the best test pilot under his command for the job. He knew the man he chose might be killed when he reached Mach 1. He also knew that if he succeeded, he would become a hero.

Chuck Yeager still enjoys the world of flying.

Chuck volunteered to fly the X-1. But he didn't think he had a chance. He was only 25 years old. Unlike most test pilots, he had never been to college. In fact, he had only recently been trained as a test pilot. But he was an excellent flier, and he stayed cool under pressure. He could hardly believe it when Colonel Boyd told him, "Okay, Yeager, it's your ride."

Colonel Boyd made the right decision. In 1947, Chuck broke the **sound barrier** in the X-1. Everyone wanted to meet Chuck. He became a national hero.

Beyond Mach 1

Chuck was **appointed** by the Air Force to direct its space-training school. His students became some of the first U.S. astronauts. Then he commanded five squadrons in the Vietnam War. Even after he retired, Chuck couldn't stay on the ground. He still tests new airplanes, flies in air shows, and sets records.

Chuck has done many dangerous things. How has he survived? Chuck says that part of it was luck. But his ability to stay cool in a **crisis** and his skill as a pilot saved his life many times. Chuck is glad that he has always gotten to do what he loves. And for Chuck, enjoying life is more important than being a hero.

Remembering Facts

Read each sentence below. Write **T** if the sentence is true. Write **F** if the sentence is false.

_____ 1. As a boy, Chuck played, hunted, and fished with the other boys.

_____ 2. Chuck grew up in West Virginia.

_____ 3. The first time Chuck rode in a plane, he loved it.

_____ 4. After combat, Chuck became a test pilot for the Air Force.

_____ 5. Chuck Yeager went to college for a short time.

_____ 6. Colonel Boyd chose Chuck for the X-1 mission.

_____ 7. Chuck's mission to fly the X-1 was delayed because of his broken ribs.

_____ 8. Chuck commanded five squadrons in the Vietnam War.

_____ 9. Chuck has the ability to stay cool in a crisis.

_____ 10. After he retired, Chuck never flew again.

Finding the Sequence

Write **1** before the sentence that tells what happened first in the story. Write **2** before the sentence that tells what happened next, and so on.

_____ Chuck signed up to serve in World War II.

_____ Chuck was shot down over enemy territory.

_____ Chuck commanded five squadrons in the Vietnam War.

_____ Chuck broke the sound barrier.

_____ Chuck became an airplane mechanic.

Using Context

Write the correct word in each blank. Choose from the words below. Use each word only once.

    later   sound   faster   speed
    never   years   crashed   grew

Chuck Yeager _____(1)_____ up in Hamlin, West Virginia. He had _____(2)_____ seen an airplane until the day one _____(3)_____ in a cornfield near town. He was 15 _____(4)_____ old.

Ten years _____(5)_____, this boy from the West Virginia hills broke the _____(6)_____ barrier. He flew _____(7)_____ than the _____(8)_____ of sound!

Drawing Conclusions

Finish each sentence by writing the best answer.

1. People outside the West Virginia hills had trouble understanding Chuck because _____
   _____

2. Chuck signed up for pilot training because _____
   _____
   _____

3. Chuck didn't think he had a chance to fly the X-1 because _____
   _____
   _____

4. Chuck has survived doing many dangerous things because _____
   _____
   _____

Identifying Facts and Opinions

Write **F** before each statement that is a fact. Write **O** before each statement that is an opinion.

_____ 1. Chuck Yeager grew up in West Virginia.

_____ 2. The first time he saw an airplane, Chuck was 15.

_____ 3. Hamlin is the prettiest town in West Virginia.

_____ 4. The world outside the West Virginia hills seemed strange to Chuck.

_____ 5. The first time Chuck rode in a plane, he got sick.

_____ 6. Chuck should have gone home after he was shot down.

_____ 7. Chuck broke the sound barrier in 1947.

_____ 8. Chuck fought in the Vietnam War.

_____ 9. Chuck is the luckiest pilot in the Air Force.

_____ 10. Chuck has done many dangerous things.

Writing Your Ideas

Colonel Boyd's decision was very hard. He knew the X-1 mission could make a man a hero, but it could also kill him. Pretend you are Colonel Boyd. Write three or four sentences about the way you feel having to make this decision.

_____

_____

_____

_____

_____

_____

Using Vocabulary

Use each of the following words in a sentence. Show by your sentence that you understand the meaning of the word. If you need help, use the Glossary.

1. speedometer

2. Mach 1

3. recruiter

4. rank

5. sound barrier

6. combat

7. appoint

8. crisis

9. ace pilot

10. mission

Grandma Fuji

It was 1 A.M. Hulda Crooks began climbing the last leg of Mount Fuji. The cold wind howled around her. But she continued up the steep, slippery side of the Japanese mountain. An hour before sunrise, she made it to the top. She passed between two stone lions. They stood for courage. A 15-foot-long banner welcomed her. It read: "You Made It, Grandma Fuji — a New Record at 91."

Expect the Unexpected

Hulda's life has been filled with the **unexpected**. "I have a **unique** old age," she says. At an age when most people start slowing down, Hulda was just getting started. She began climbing mountains at 66. By the end of 1986, she had climbed to the top of 97 mountains in California. Among them was Mount Whitney, the tallest mountain in the United States outside of Alaska. Hulda has climbed Mount Whitney 22 times.

Hulda became famous for mountain climbing. She is also well-known outside the U.S. Hulda has been on TV and in newspapers all over the world. A Japanese company invited her to climb Mount Fuji. Every year the company's employees get together and climb the mountain. The company paid for Hulda's trip to Japan so she could join them. About 20 television crews and news organizations covered the event.

In July of 1987, Hulda became the oldest woman to climb to the top of Mount Fuji. She was 91 years old. When asked if she planned to do it again, she said no. But then she said, "I've learned never to **predict** what I will do. All sorts of wonderful things happen that you could never quite expect. That's what makes life exciting."

A Healthy Change

Born in 1896, Hulda grew up on a farm in Saskatchewan, Canada. By age 18, she'd finished only five grades in school. Hulda wanted to continue her education, but her father didn't agree. So she left home and went to live in a **boarding school**. Hulda paid for her education by working in the kitchen. She also sold books door-to-door.

As a teenager, Hulda was overweight. Then she joined a church that taught its members to eat a **vegetarian** diet. Hulda follows this teaching. She believes this diet has helped her stay healthy.

In 1923, Hulda moved to Loma Linda, California. She went to college and studied **dietetics**. Soon Hulda married a college professor. He was the one who **encouraged** Hulda to take up mountain climbing.

It's Never Too Late

"It's never too early, but it's also never too late," says Hulda. Hulda started late with her exercise program. She began jogging at 70 after she read about its **benefits**. Hulda wasn't discouraged by her age. She is a **determined** person.

Hulda lives an active life. She gives talks on physical fitness. She tells people to take **responsibility** for their health. "Human beings are allowed only one body per customer," she says. Hulda believes that most people don't take care of themselves the way they should. Then when they get sick, they expect a doctor to cure them. Hulda feels that regular exercise, a good diet, and a peaceful mind are the secrets of her long life.

Hulda especially likes talking to older people. She tells them they must show others that life is worth living. "It's up to us to keep our light shining and our banner flying until the last breath," she says.

Remembering Facts

In the blank, write the letter of the best ending for each sentence.

_____ 1. Hulda Crooks was born in
 a. Germany.   b. Canada.   c. Japan.

_____ 2. At age 91, Hulda became the oldest woman to climb to the top of
 a. Mount Fuji.   b. Mount Whitney.   c. Mount Everest.

_____ 3. Hulda began climbing mountains when she was
 a. 70.   b. 18.   c. 66.

_____ 4. Hulda says that one of the secrets of her long life is
 a. regular exercise.   b. regular checkups.
 c. a diet of steak and hamburgers.

_____ 5. Hulda learned to eat a vegetarian diet
 a. in a diet center.   b. in a health spa.
 c. when she joined a church.

_____ 6. In college, Hulda studied
 a. dietetics.   b. medicine.   c. business.

_____ 7. Hulda climbed Mount Fuji in
 a. 1986.   b. 1987.   c. 1985.

_____ 8. Hulda especially likes talking to
 a. reporters.   b. older people.   c. younger people.

Finding the Sequence

Write **1** before the sentence that tells what happened first in the story. Write **2** before the sentence that tells what happened next, and so on.

_____ Hulda went to college.

_____ Hulda climbed to the top of Mount Fuji.

_____ Hulda went to live in a boarding school.

_____ Hulda began climbing mountains.

_____ Hulda began jogging.

Using Context

Write the correct word in each blank. Choose from the words below. Use each word only once.

    health   woman   learn   people
    age   enjoyed   late   old

Hulda Crooks is an amazing _____(1)_____. Young and _____(2)_____ people have much to _____(3)_____ from her. In her old _____(4)_____, she has done things that many young _____(5)_____ would never dream of doing. And she has _____(6)_____ every minute! She encourages others to take responsibility for their _____(7)_____. She says it is never too _____(8)_____.

Drawing Conclusions

Finish each sentence by writing the best answer.

1. Hulda left home and went to live in a boarding school because _____

2. Hulda says she has a unique old age because _____

3. Hulda has learned never to predict what she will do because _____

4. Hulda especially likes talking to older people because _____

39

Identifying Facts and Opinions

Write **F** before each statement that is a fact. Write **O** before each statement that is an opinion.

_____ 1. Hulda shouldn't risk her life the way she does.

_____ 2. A vegetarian diet is better than a diet that includes meat.

_____ 3. Hulda Crooks grew up on a farm in Canada.

_____ 4. Hulda married a college professor.

_____ 5. Hulda has climbed Mount Whitney 22 times.

_____ 6. Hulda Crooks is the most daring woman in this book.

_____ 7. A Japanese company invited Hulda to climb Mount Fuji.

_____ 8. Hulda climbed to the top of Mount Fuji in 1987.

_____ 9. Everybody should climb mountains at an old age.

_____ 10. Hulda Crooks is a vegetarian.

Writing Your Ideas

Hulda Crooks says, "Human beings are allowed only one body per customer." What do you think she is trying to tell us? Write three or four sentences about what you think.

Using Vocabulary

Write the correct word in each sentence.

benefit	vegetarian	unexpected
determined	unique	encourage
predict	responsibility	dietetics
boarding school		

1. A school where students can live is a ———————————.

2. To tell in advance is to ———————————.

3. To make your own choices about important matters is to take ———————————.

4. Something that is very unusual or uncommon is ———————————.

5. The science that deals with the amount and kind of food needed by the body is called ———————————.

6. A diet based mainly on vegetables is a ——————————— diet.

7. Something that happens without warning is ———————————.

8. When you give someone hope, confidence, and courage, you ——————————— her or him.

9. Something that helps a person or thing is a ———————————.

10. When you know what you want and work to accomplish it, you are a ——————————— person.

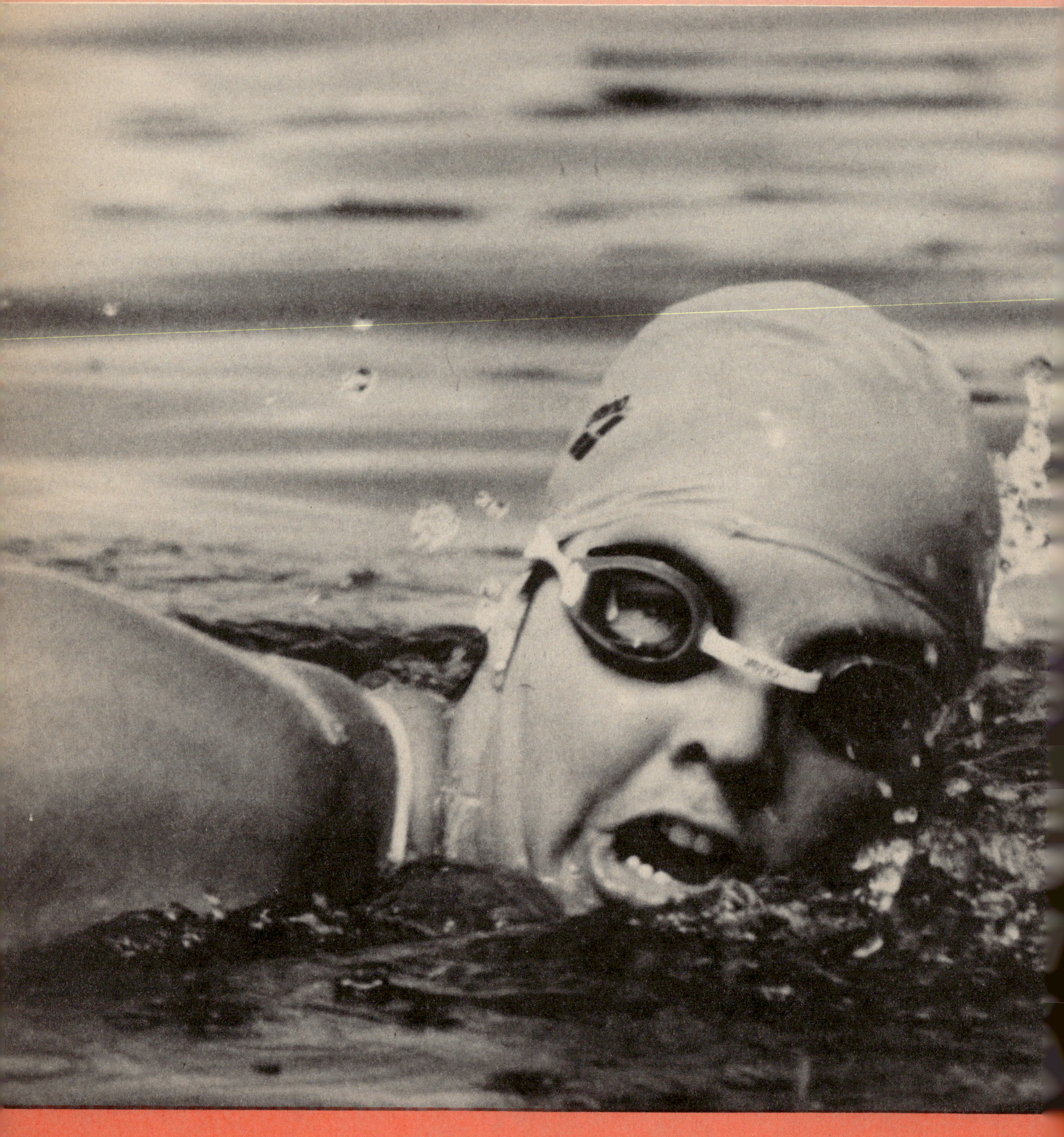

The Impossible Swim

The icy sea churned like a washing machine. Lynne was tired and cold. Her toes were numb and her hands stung as if they were on fire. "I was feeling really bad," Lynne remembers, "and suddenly the **dolphins** appeared. They swam up to me. They kept me company." The dolphins helped give Lynne the courage to finish her amazing swim.

Cold Enough to Kill

Long-distance swimmer Lynne Cox set a new record for ocean swimming. Lynne completed the longest cold-water swim in history. She spent two hours and six minutes in 44-degree water. It was cold enough to kill the average person in 30 minutes!

Lynne swam across the Bering Strait, from the coast of Alaska to a Russian island. The Russians hadn't allowed any Americans to come to that island since 1948. Lynne was met by a Russian welcoming committee. Sports officials and reporters cheered for her and gave her flowers.

Lynne made the swim to encourage better feelings between Russia and the United States. Also, she wanted to help scientists learn more about how **extreme** cold affects people. "I've been getting into cold water for a long time," says Lynne, "so I said to myself, 'Why not let someone else **benefit**?'"

Lynne did what many thought was impossible. "Tell me I can't do something, and my **attitude** is I'll do it," she says. Lynne has proven her claim true.

Breaking Records

Lynne began setting long-distance swimming records when she was just 15. That year she swam the English Channel. She broke both the men's and women's speed records. At age 18, she became the first woman to swim New Zealand's Cook Strait.

But Lynne wasn't always a success at swimming. She tried competitive pool swimming and failed. "I wasn't good at it," she says. "I didn't have the speed." So she switched to long-distance swimming. "You always have the challenge of the **elements** to deal with," she says. "I love it."

Over the years, Lynne worked to succeed at her sport. She trained hard for her swim to Russia. She swam in the Pacific Ocean six days a week, three hours a day.

Lynne wanted to make sure she was ready for the **frigid** waters of the Bering Strait. She made a trip to Glacier Bay, Alaska. A guide boat broke up sheets of

Russian officials welcome Lynne to their island.

ice so she could swim. Lynne stayed in the water for 30 minutes! But when she was ready, Lynne had to wait. The Russian government took a year to **approve** her swim to their island.

Nature's Challenge

Lynne finally made her swim in August, 1987. Nature was her biggest challenge. Sharks, heavy tides, and strong **currents** threatened her safety. Then there was the cold water, only 12 degrees above freezing. "It was the riskiest, most frightening, most difficult thing I've ever done," says Lynne.

Lynne didn't wear a wet suit to protect her from the cold. She had only her body fat to keep her warm. Fortunately, Lynne carried 190 pounds of muscle and fat on her 5'6" frame.

She swam as quickly as she could. "I was swimming faster than I ever swam before," Lynne says. "I had to move as fast as I could to **generate** heat." Several times, she felt so bad she was afraid she couldn't finish. But her friends urged her on.

Lynne is glad she didn't give up. "It was one of those rare **occasions** in life when things turn out better than you ever imagined," she says. "And I could see from the eyes of the Russians that it was special for them, too."

Remembering Facts

Read each sentence below. Write **T** if the sentence is true. Write **F** if the sentence is false.

_____ 1. Lynne Cox swam the English Channel when she was 15 years old.

_____ 2. Lynne is very good at competitive swimming.

_____ 3. Lynne loves the challenge of the elements.

_____ 4. The Russian government took a year to approve Lynne's swim to their island.

_____ 5. To prepare for her swim to Russia, Lynne swam in the Caribbean Sea six days a week.

_____ 6. The longest cold-water swim in history took two hours and six minutes.

_____ 7. Lynne swam across the Bering Strait in 1987.

_____ 8. Lynne wore a wet suit when she swam across the Bering Strait.

_____ 9. The swim across the Bering Strait was easy.

_____ 10. It was easy for Lynne to swim in very cold water because she was so thin.

Finding the Sequence

Write **1** before the sentence that tells what happened first in the story. Write **2** before the sentence that tells what happened next, and so on.

_____ Lynne swam across the Bering Strait.

_____ Lynne swam New Zealand's Cook Strait.

_____ Lynne switched from competitive pool swimming to long-distance swimming.

_____ Lynne began setting long-distance swimming records.

_____ Lynne made a trip to Glacier Bay, Alaska.

Using Context

Write the correct word in each blank. Choose from the words below. Use each word only once.

swim	appeared	her	finish
were	animals	she	too

Dolphins are very intelligent _____(1)_____. And if you ask Lynne Cox, she'll probably tell you they are friendly, _____(2)_____. They _____(3)_____ very kind to her on her _____(4)_____ across the Bering Strait. Just when _____(5)_____ was feeling really bad, the dolphins _____(6)_____. They kept _____(7)_____ company. They gave her courage to _____(8)_____ her swim.

Drawing Conclusions

Finish each sentence by writing the best answer.

1. Lynne made the swim across the Bering Strait because _____

2. When Lynne was ready for her swim, she had to wait because _____

3. Lynne made a trip to Glacier Bay, Alaska, because _____

4. In her swim across the Bering Strait, Lynne had to move as fast as she could because _____

Identifying Facts and Opinions

Write **F** before each statement that is a fact. Write **O** before each statement that is an opinion.

_____ 1. Lynne Cox spent two hours and six minutes in 44-degree water.

_____ 2. Lynne began setting records when she was 15 years old.

_____ 3. Lynne should have worn a wet suit to protect her body from the cold.

_____ 4. Lynne swam New Zealand's Cook Strait at age 18.

_____ 5. It was very nice of the Russians to approve Lynne's swim.

_____ 6. Lynne should have crossed the Bering Strait by boat.

_____ 7. Lynne weighed 190 pounds when she swam the Bering Strait.

_____ 8. It was foolish of Lynne to continue swimming after her toes got numb.

_____ 9. Lynne swam the Bering Strait in August, 1987.

_____ 10. Lynne's attitude towards life is better than most people's.

Writing Your Ideas

We're all better at some things than at others. Lynne tried competitive pool swimming and failed. But she switched to long-distance swimming and started setting records. Write about something you feel you do really well.

_____
_____
_____
_____
_____

Using Vocabulary

Use each of the following words in a sentence. Show by your sentence that you understand the meaning of the word. If you need help, use the Glossary.

1. approve
2. current
3. elements
4. attitude
5. dolphin
6. frigid
7. extreme
8. benefit
9. occasion
10. generate

Man in Motion

Three hundred people were gathered in the parking lot. They stood out in the wind and rain to wish Rick Hansen a safe journey. Rick was leaving on a long trip, but it wasn't a vacation. It was his Man in Motion World Tour. He was going to push himself around the world in his **wheelchair**! Two years later, a crowd of 7,000 people waited for him at the same parking lot. They cheered the arrival of the man who wouldn't give up.

51

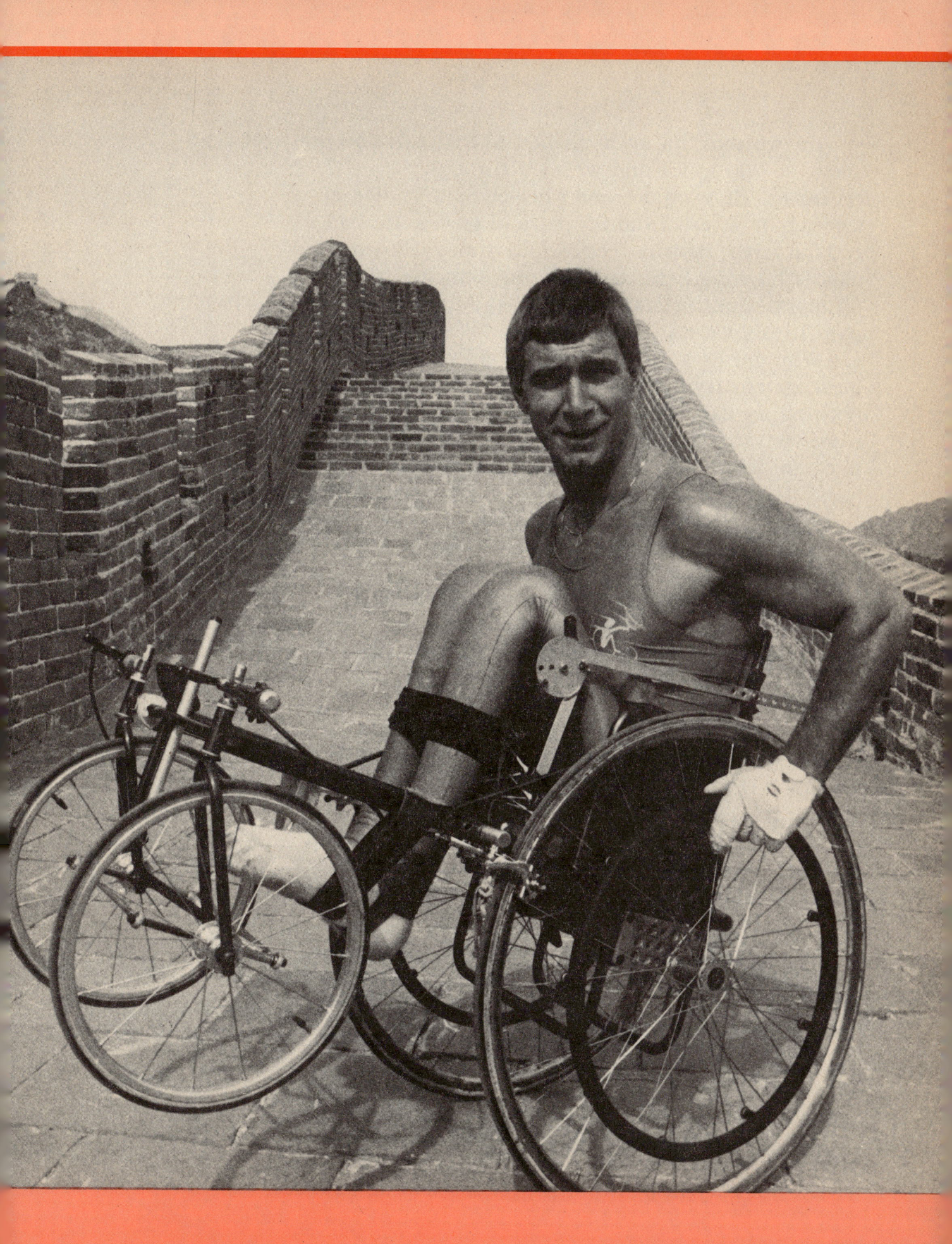

A Message of Hope

In two years, a lot happened to Rick. He covered about 25,000 miles and wheeled through 34 countries. He wore out one wheelchair, five sets of wheelchair wheels, and 95 pairs of gloves. He had 100 flat tires. He was robbed four times. He survived floods, burning heat, and freezing cold. He wheeled up mountains, including the Swiss Alps. He suffered pain in his wrists, back, and shoulders.

Why did Rick do it? He had a mission. "The message I'm trying to get across is that there is nothing we can't do, if we set our minds to it," he says. He wanted others to see the **potential** of people like him who have **disabilities**. "The fact is," Rick says, "that I have now made myself **accomplish** things I might never have done if I had not had the accident."

Wheelchair Athlete

Rick was born in 1957 in British Columbia, Canada. At age 15, he lost the use of his legs. He was hitchhiking home from a fishing trip. He got a ride in the back of a pickup truck. He was thrown out and broke his back.

His doctors told him he'd never be able to use his legs again. At first he didn't believe them. Then he became angry and bitter about what had happened. Finally, he decided to get on with living.

Always a good **athlete**, Rick wanted to be a top wheelchair athlete. While in high school, he competed in wheelchair sports, including **marathons**. He was the first person with a physical disability to get a degree in physical education from the University of British Columbia.

By 1981, Rick had become one of the world's top wheelchair athletes. He was one of two athletes named Canada's Outstanding Athlete of the Year in 1983.

A Sense of Pride

But Rick wanted to do more. He wanted to wheel himself around the world. His friends thought he was crazy, but they helped him. In 1985, Rick, age 27, set out on his trip with a crew of four. He left from Vancouver, British Columbia, where he lived.

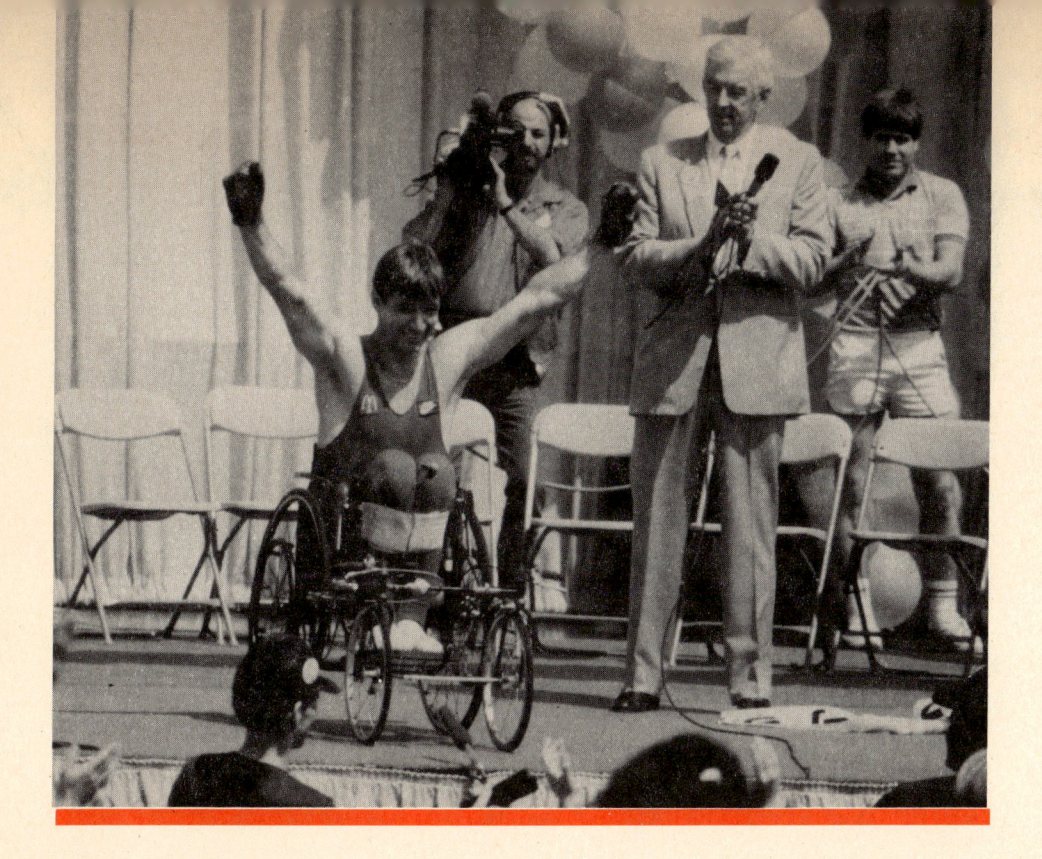

At one point, Rick and his crew almost ran out of money. But people heard about what he was doing and gave him **donations**. Companies such as Nike, McDonald's, and Safeway helped, too. Rick's trip was paid for, and he had money left over. By the end of the trip, he'd raised seven million dollars to help people with disabilities.

But Rick helped people with disabilities by giving them more than money. He also gave them pride. When Rick was in Poland, several men in wheelchairs followed him. They wheeled with him as he went into a town. "Probably for the first time in their lives, they were proud to be in a wheelchair," says Rick.

Rick helped people without disabilities, too. Rick told this story about one of them. In New Mexico, a man with tears in his eyes came up to Rick. The man said, "I just lost my business, and I was thinking about **suicide**. I just didn't know where to turn. Then I heard about you and realized it's not the end for me. It's just time to rise to new challenges."

Rick made a difference to this man and many others. As Rick once said, "We should be the best we can with what we have."

Remembering Facts

In the blank, write the letter of the best ending for each sentence.

_____ 1. Rick Hansen was born in
   a. Toronto.   b. British Columbia.   c. Montreal.

_____ 2. Rick lost the use of his legs at age
   a. 27.   b. 18.   c. 15.

_____ 3. In college, Rick studied
   a. physical education.   b. medicine.   c. history.

_____ 4. Rick left for his Man in Motion World Tour in
   a. 1981.   b. 1983.   c. 1985.

_____ 5. By the end of the trip, Rick
   a. was ready to give up.
   b. had raised seven million dollars.
   c. decided to stay in Poland and live.

_____ 6. Rick helped many people with disabilities by giving them
   a. pride.   b. wheelchairs.   c. new gloves.

Finding the Sequence

Write **1** before the sentence that tells what happened first in the story. Write **2** before the sentence that tells what happened next, and so on.

_____ Rick set out on his trip around the world.

_____ Rick started competing in wheelchair sports.

_____ A crowd of 7,000 people cheered Rick's arrival.

_____ Rick broke his back.

_____ Rick became Canada's Outstanding Athlete of the Year.

Using Context

Write the correct word in each blank. Choose from the words below. Use each word only once.

| helped | importantly | people | with |
| lives | disabilities | raised | He |

Rick Hansen has made a difference in the _____(1)_____ of many people. He has _____(2)_____ money to help people with _____(3)_____. But more _____(4)_____, he has given these _____(5)_____ pride. Rick has _____(6)_____ people without disabilities, too. _____(7)_____ says, "We should be the best we can _____(8)_____ what we have."

Drawing Conclusions

Finish each sentence by writing the best answer.

1. Rick lost the use of his legs because _____

2. At one point, Rick and his crew almost ran out of money, but they were able to continue because _____

3. Rick made a difference to the man in New Mexico because _____

4. During his trip, Rick suffered cold, heat, and pain. He didn't give up because _____

Identifying Facts and Opinions

Write **F** before each statement that is a fact. Write **O** before each statement that is an opinion.

_____ 1. Rick was born in British Columbia.

_____ 2. Rick should have given up after he was robbed.

_____ 3. In his tour around the world, Rick wheeled through 34 countries.

_____ 4. Going around the world in a wheelchair is harder than walking around the world.

_____ 5. Nobody has helped people with disabilities more than Rick Hansen.

_____ 6. Rick got a degree in physical education from the University of British Columbia.

_____ 7. Rick and his crew received donations from people and companies.

_____ 8. Rick shouldn't have gone on that fishing trip when he was 15 years old.

_____ 9. Rick is one of the top wheelchair athletes in the world.

_____ 10. People should never give up.

Writing Your Ideas

When Rick was in Poland, several men in wheelchairs wheeled with him as he went into a town. Rick says, "Probably for the first time in their lives, they were proud to be in a wheelchair." Write three or four sentences telling why you think these men were proud.

Using Vocabulary

Use the clues to complete the puzzle. Choose from the words in the box.

wheelchair
potential
disability
marathon
donation
suicide
athlete
accomplish

Across
3. get it done
5. chair mounted on wheels
6. an ability that may or may not be developed
7. a person who is good at sports
8. a gift

Down
1. long-distance race
2. killing oneself
4. lack of ability

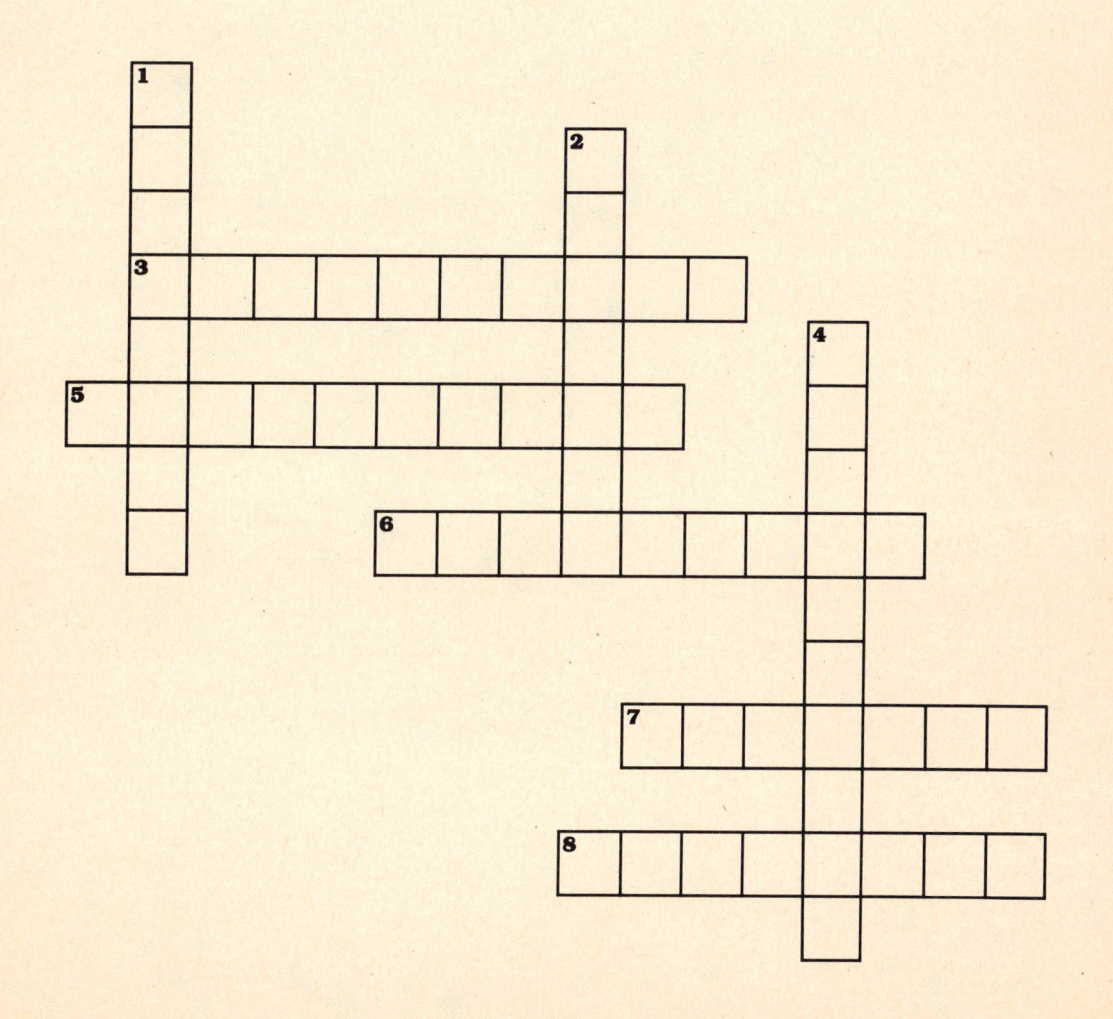

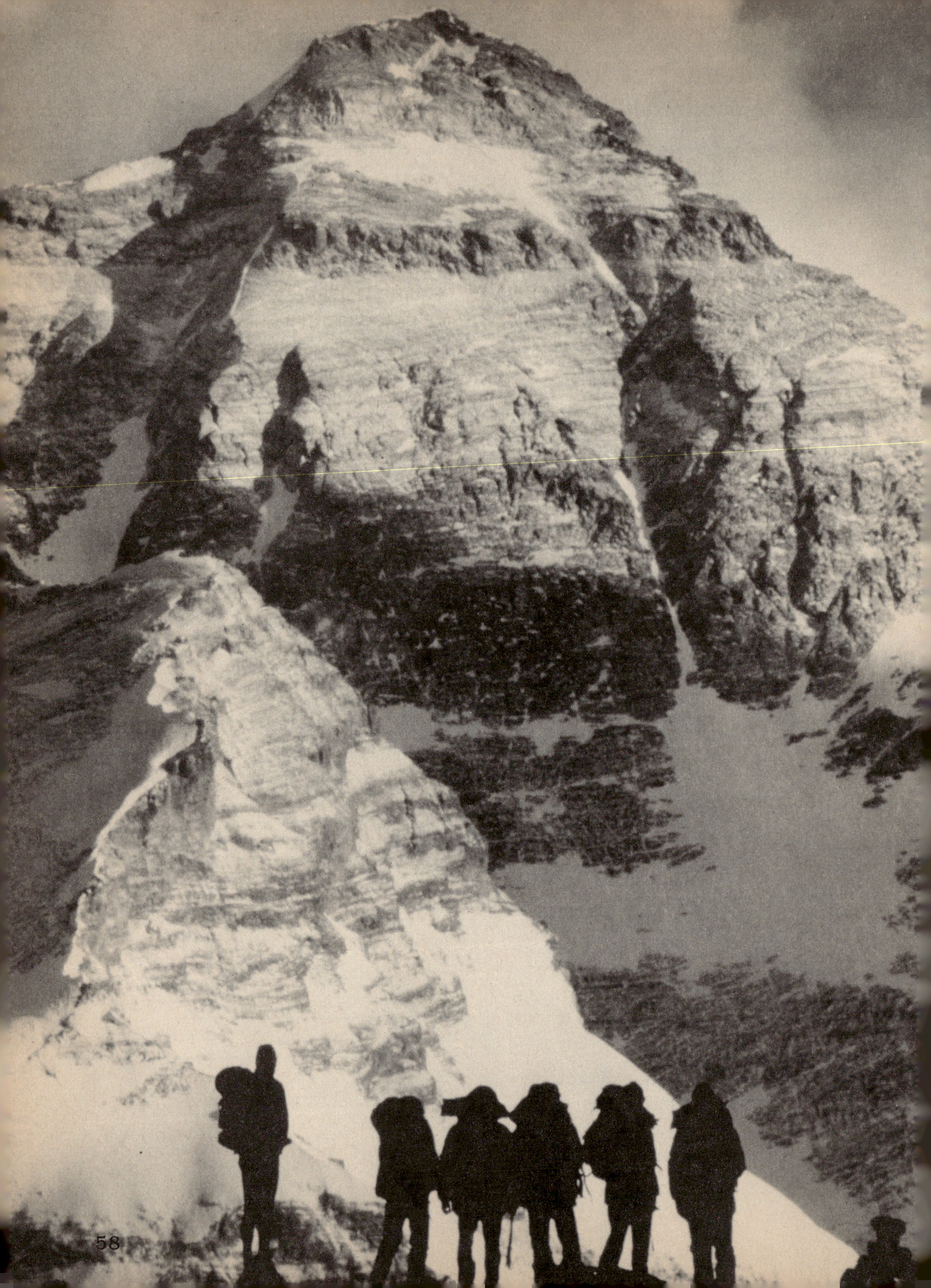

On Top of the World

On a May morning in 1953, two exhausted climbers struggled up a wall of ice. Every inch of progress took great effort. But they pushed on. The two men were driven to make history.

The Highest Point on Earth

Between India and China is a mountain range called the Himalayas. Mount Everest, the highest point on Earth, is among its peaks. Many people had tried to climb it before 1953. All had failed. Of these people, 16 died on the mountain.

For mountain climbers, Everest is the challenge of a lifetime. There is danger from **avalanches**, steep **terrain**, high winds, and extreme cold. Also, there is not much oxygen in the air towards the top. The lack of oxygen makes climbers feel tired and weak. It also affects their ability to think clearly.

In the spring of 1953, **veteran** climber John Hunt organized the eighth **expedition** to climb Mount Everest. This expedition had an advantage over earlier expeditions. Lighter oxygen tanks had been developed. Now climbers could carry oxygen for use in the higher **elevations**.

Reaching for the Summit

One of the members of the Hunt expedition was Edmund Hillary. Edmund was born in New Zealand in 1919. He made his living as a beekeeper. But his real love was climbing mountains. He began going on expeditions to the Himalayas and became an experienced climber. In the early 1950's, he made two trips partway up Mount Everest.

Also on the expedition was Tenzing Norgay. Tenzing grew up at the foot of the Himalayas. He was a **porter** with the Hunt expedition. Tenzing began working with Everest expeditions when he was just 19 years old.

After two months of hard work, Edmund, Tenzing, and the others set up camp 3,200 feet below Everest's peak. Finally it was time to try for the **summit**. The climbers went in pairs. The first pair came within 300 feet of their goal. But they were too tired to continue.

On May 28th, Edmund set out for the summit with his partner, Tenzing. At 27,900 feet, Edmund and Tenzing set up camp for the night. The **gusty** wind threatened to blow their tent away. The two men ate a supper of sardines, crackers, dates, and honey in their sleeping bags. Then they dozed and waited for dawn.

Everest Conquered

At nine the next morning, Edmund and Tenzing found themselves faced with a challenge. They stood at the foot of a 40-foot-high wall of snow. Edmund cut steps in the snow, and they started up. Suddenly part of the snow gave way, and they slid partway down. They knew it was dangerous to go further. They could easily be buried in an avalanche. But they decided to take the risk. Soon the snow became firmer. They came to the top of the wall and struggled slowly on.

"Suddenly," Edmund wrote in his **diary**, "I realize that the ridge ahead doesn't slope up, but down. I look quickly to my right. There, just above me, is a softly rounded, snow-covered little bump about as big as a haystack — the summit."

Edmund tested the snow to see if it was firm. Then he and Tenzing climbed to the top of the world. Later, Edmund wrote about that moment. "I feel relief and a sense of wonder. I turn to Tenzing and shake his hand. He throws his arms around my shoulders, and there is very little we can say or need to say."

Edmund took pictures to prove they had reached the summit. Then the two men climbed carefully back down to camp. They told the rest of the expedition that Everest had been conquered. Edmund and Tenzing were heroes! When Edmund returned home, he was **knighted** by Queen Elizabeth. The beekeeper from New Zealand had become Sir Edmund Hillary.

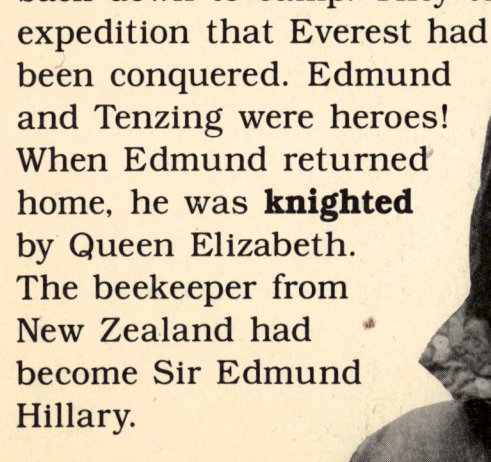

Remembering Facts

Read each sentence below. Write **T** if the sentence is true. Write **F** if the sentence is false.

_____ 1. Edmund Hillary was born in New Zealand.

_____ 2. The Himalayas are between India and China.

_____ 3. Edmund Hillary's real love has always been beekeeping.

_____ 4. Tenzing Norgay began working with Everest expeditions when he was 19 years old.

_____ 5. Mount Everest is an easy peak to climb.

_____ 6. In the spring of 1953, John Hunt organized the first expedition to climb Mount Everest.

_____ 7. Tenzing was a porter with the Hunt expedition.

_____ 8. Edmund and Tenzing made history on a May morning in 1953.

_____ 9. Edmund took pictures to prove Tenzing and he had reached the summit.

_____ 10. When Edmund returned home, he was ignored by everybody.

Finding the Sequence

Write **1** before the sentence that tells what happened first in the story. Write **2** before the sentence that tells what happened next, and so on.

_____ Edmund and Tenzing reached the summit of Mount Everest.

_____ The Hunt expedition set up a camp 3,200 feet below Everest's peak.

_____ Edmund and Tenzing stood at the foot of a 40-foot-high wall of snow.

_____ Edmund was knighted by Queen Elizabeth.

_____ Edmund Hillary made two trips partway up Mount Everest.

Using Context

Write the correct word in each blank. Choose from the words below. Use each word only once.

heroes	climbed	by	and
they	mountain	top	Mount

Can you imagine standing on _____(1)_____ of the world? Edmund Hillary _____(2)_____ Tenzing Norgay did it in 1953. They _____(3)_____ to the top of the highest _____(4)_____ in the world. They conquered _____(5)_____ Everest! This had been tried _____(6)_____ many people before. But _____(7)_____ all had failed. After Edmund and Tenzing finally reached the summit, they became _____(8)_____.

Drawing Conclusions

Finish each sentence by writing the best answer.

1. For mountain climbers, Mount Everest is the challenge of a lifetime because _____

_____

2. Towards the top of Mount Everest, climbers cannot think clearly because _____

3. The members of the Hunt expedition had an advantage over earlier climbers because _____

_____

4. When Edmund and Tenzing reached the summit, there was very little they needed to say because _____

_____

63

Identifying Facts and Opinions

Write **F** before each statement that is a fact. Write **O** before each statement that is an opinion.

_____ 1. Tenzing Norgay grew up at the foot of the Himalayas.

_____ 2. Nobody should have tried to climb Mount Everest before 1953.

_____ 3. Edmund Hillary was a beekeeper.

_____ 4. Edmund and Tenzing were the bravest men on the Hunt expedition.

_____ 5. Edmund Hillary was knighted by Queen Elizabeth.

_____ 6. Climbing a mountain is really not that difficult.

_____ 7. Mount Everest is the highest point on Earth.

_____ 8. The lack of oxygen makes climbers feel tired and weak.

_____ 9. There is nothing like the feeling you get when you reach the summit of a mountain.

_____ 10. Mountain climbing is more dangerous than auto racing.

Writing Your Ideas

Edmund Hillary and Tenzing Norgay stood on top of the world in 1953. What is the most exciting or interesting place you've been to? Write three or four sentences about that place.

Using Vocabulary

Write the correct word in each sentence.

| avalanche | porter | knighted | gusty | terrain |
| elevation | summit | veteran | diary | expedition |

1. A journey that has a special purpose is an _____.

2. A person who carries heavy things for other people is called a _____.

3. The height above the surface of Earth is called _____.

4. The highest point of a mountain is its _____.

5. A large mass of snow that comes down a mountainside is an _____.

6. Another word for ground is _____.

7. A person with much experience is a _____.

8. When a man is _____, he is honored for doing a service to his country.

9. A written record is a _____.

10. Wind that has sudden rushes of air is called _____.

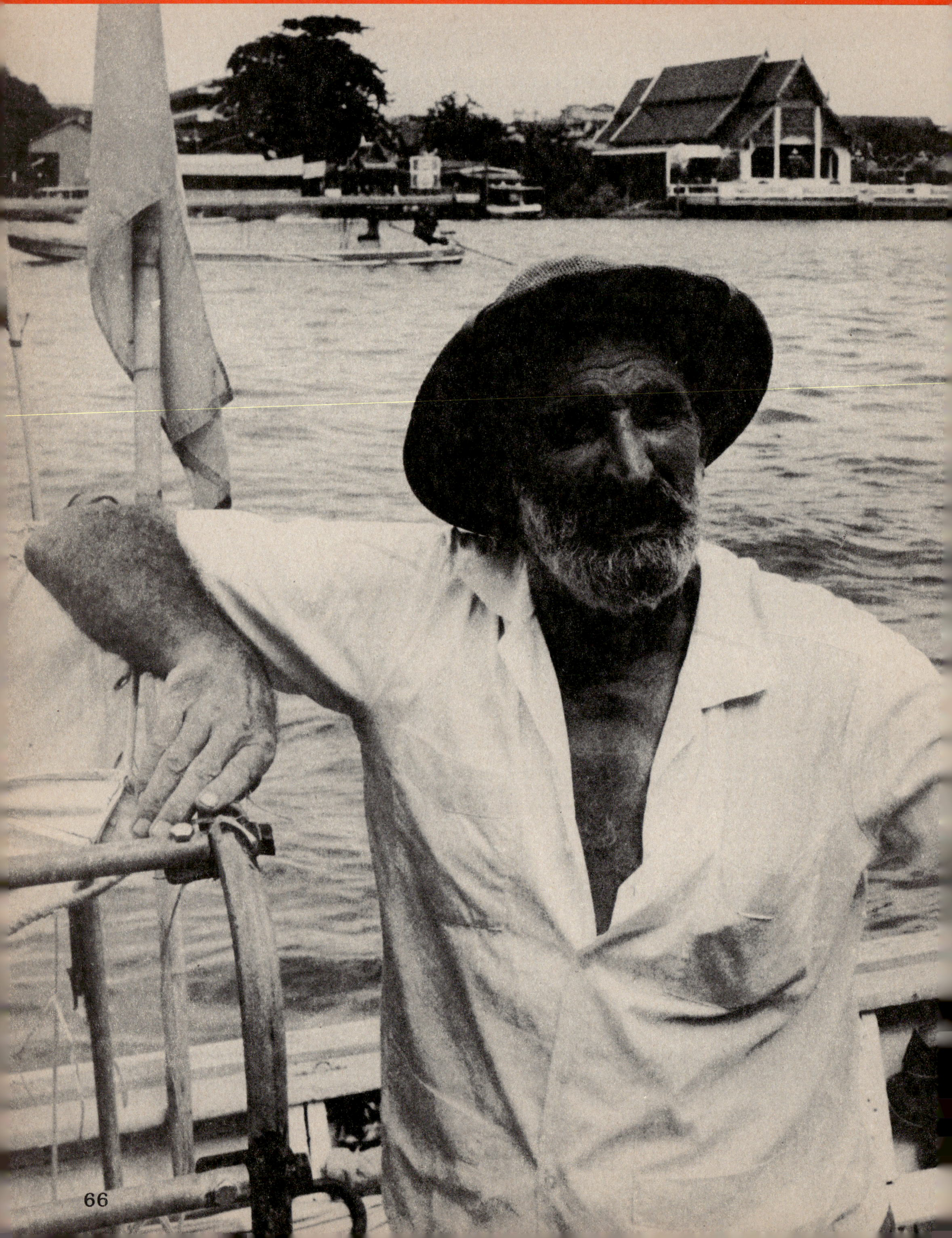

The Voyage of *Outward Leg*

Tristan Jones was standing on the deck of his **trimaran**. Suddenly, he heard a loud splash. Tristan looked into the water and saw a huge head looking back at him. It was an enormous whale! The whale could easily have **capsized** the small boat. For two terrible hours, the whale played around the trimaran. Finally it swam some distance away. Then it rushed straight toward the trimaran! At the last minute, the whale dove under the boat and disappeared into the ocean. For Tristan Jones, it was only one day in a lifetime filled with adventure.

Born to Sail

Tristan Jones was born on a ship. His father was the captain. Tristan grew up in Wales, a part of Great Britain. His family lived in a village by the sea. Tristan was only 14 when he left home to start his own sailing career. He worked as a deck boy. Then, when World War II began, Tristan joined the British Royal Navy.

After the war, Tristan made many voyages. He set nine world records for sailing **craft** that were less than 40 feet long. He sailed across the Atlantic Ocean 18 times and around the world three times. Tristan made his living by writing books and giving lectures about his adventures.

A New Challenge

In 1982, Tristan was in Amsterdam, Holland. One day, he was standing on the sidewalk. Suddenly he felt a terrible pain in his leg. He fell right in front of a streetcar! Luckily, the driver managed to stop.

Tristan went back home to New York. He **collapsed** again. His doctor told him that some old injuries from World War II had stopped the flow of blood in his left leg. His leg had to be **amputated**.

In the hospital, Tristan met other people who had had amputations. Many of them were young, and many of them were **depressed**. They saw no hope for the future. "Some of them died while I was there because they had no reason to live," remembers Tristan, "and that I refuse to accept."

Tristan made a promise to himself. He decided to prove that having a disability wasn't the end of the world. He would go back to sea and sail around the world!

Tristan wrote three books and started lecturing again. Soon he had enough money to begin planning his voyage. He called it "Operation Star."

Operation Star

Tristan knew that some adjustments had to be made because he had lost his leg. A boat with three

hulls would be much more stable than a regular boat and easier to move around on. So Tristan began looking for a trimaran.

One day Tristan got an offer to give a lecture in San Diego, California. While in San Diego, Tristan found the perfect trimaran. It was just what he wanted. But he couldn't afford it.

Then Tristan met some people who had read his books. They had heard about Operation Star, and they wanted to help. They also wanted to prove that trimarans make good ocean-going boats. So they bought the trimaran and let Tristan use it. Tristan named his new boat *Outward Leg*.

On October 17, 1983, Tristan set out with his crew aboard *Outward Leg*. Wherever they went, adventure followed. At sea, they fought **severe** storms. Large ships threatened to run over the little boat. When they landed, Tristan and his crew had to watch out for thieves and **smugglers**.

But Tristan's dream was coming true. He received letters from other people with disabilities. They knew about what he was doing and admired his courage. These letters gave Tristan the strength to continue. "I'm not in this for thrills," he says. "I'm doing it to give hope to people who've been disabled like me, especially the young people."

There is an ancient Welsh **myth** about a king named Mannanan. He was a great warrior who had only one leg. Tristan has adopted Mannanan's motto: "Whichever way you turn me, I will stand."

Remembering Facts

In the blank, write the letter of the best ending for each sentence.

_____ 1. Tristan Jones was born on a
   a. ship.   b. farm.   c. train.

_____ 2. Tristan's family lived in a village by the
   a. mountains.   b. jungle.   c. sea.

_____ 3. Tristan started his sailing career at age
   a. 14.   b. 40.   c. 24.

_____ 4. When World War II began, Tristan
   a. ran away.   b. joined the British Royal Navy.
   c. moved to the United States.

_____ 5. After the war, Tristan sailed around the world
   a. once.   b. 18 times.   c. three times.

_____ 6. The day Tristan fell in front of a street car,
   a. the driver stopped just in time.   b. he broke his arm.
   c. he lost his leg.

_____ 7. Tristan called his voyage around the world
   a. *Outward Leg.*   b. "Operation Star."   c. "Mannanan."

_____ 8. Whenever Tristan Jones and his crew landed, they had to watch out for
   a. wild animals.   b. thieves.   c. children throwing rocks.

Finding the Sequence

Write **1** before the sentence that tells what happened first in the story. Write **2** before the sentence that tells what happened next, and so on.

_____ Tristan set out with his crew aboard *Outward Leg.*

_____ Tristan left home to start his own sailing career.

_____ Tristan fell in front of a streetcar.

_____ Tristan joined the British Royal Navy.

_____ Tristan's leg was amputated.

Using Context

Write the correct word in each blank. Choose from the words below. Use each word only once.

minute	it	nothing	enormous
toward	a	whale	spent

There ___(1)___ was. An ___(2)___ whale looking at him! Tristan knew the ___(3)___ could have capsized the boat. But there was ___(4)___ to do but wait. The whale ___(5)___ two hours playing around the trimaran. Suddenly, the whale rushed ___(6)___ the boat. It was ___(7)___ terrifying moment! Luckily, at the last ___(8)___, the whale dove under the boat and left.

Drawing Conclusions

Finish each sentence by writing the best answer.

1. Tristan's left leg had to be amputated because _____

2. In the hospital, Tristan met other people who had had amputations. He says some of them died because _____

3. Tristan thought a trimaran would be better for his voyage because _____

4. Tristan didn't decide to sail around the world for thrills. He decided to do it because _____

71

Identifying Facts and Opinions

Write **F** before each statement that is a fact. Write **O** before each statement that is an opinion.

_____ 1. Tristan Jones grew up in Wales.

_____ 2. Tristan's father was the captain of a ship.

_____ 3. Growing up in a village by the sea would be boring.

_____ 4. Tristan went to work as a deck boy when he was 14 years old.

_____ 5. After the war, Tristan sailed across the Atlantic Ocean 18 times.

_____ 6. Tristan is the bravest person in this book.

_____ 7. People who have had an amputation shouldn't get depressed.

_____ 8. Trimarans are better than other boats.

_____ 9. Amsterdam is in Holland.

_____ 10. *Outward Leg* is a good name for a boat.

Writing Your Ideas

Tristan saw that some people who had had an amputation died because they had no hope for the future. He decided to prove that having a disability wasn't the end of the world. Do you think "Operation Star" has helped him prove this? Write three or four sentences telling whether you think this voyage was a good idea.

_____

_____

_____

_____

_____

Using Vocabulary

Use each of the following words in a sentence. Show by your sentence that you understand the meaning of the word. If you need help, use the Glossary.

1. trimaran

2. craft

3. amputate

4. capsize

5. collapse

6. smuggler

7. depressed

8. severe

9. hull

10. myth

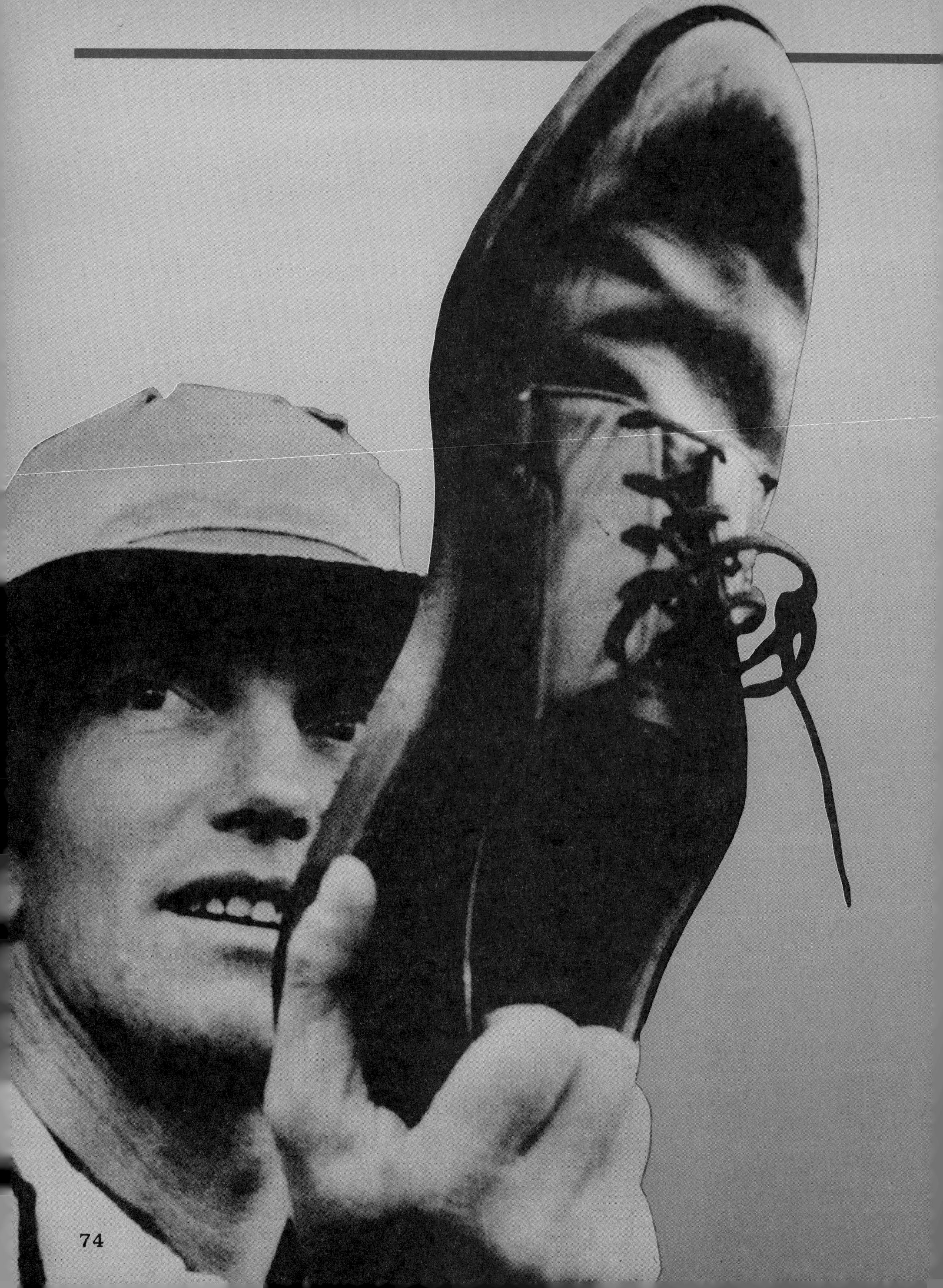

A Long Walk

On October 21, 1972, David and John Kunst were camping in Afghanistan. They were reading by candlelight when suddenly they heard gunfire. David and John were both hit! Bandits came into their camp and started searching for money. David lay very still. "I was shot in the chest," he remembers, "and the bandits might have finished me off, but I played dead." Finally the bandits left. David was safe. But John had been killed.

Something Different

David Kunst led an ordinary life. He lived in a small town. In the daytime, he headed a county **survey crew**. At night, he worked as a **projectionist** at a theater. But David was bored. "I made up my mind that I would do something that would be a little different. I wanted an adventure in my life. So I just walked out of town." David kept walking all the way around the world!

In July of 1970, David recorded the first steps of his journey in wet cement in front of the theater in his hometown of Waseca, Minnesota. Then he started out with his brother John and a mule named Willie Make-It. The mule was a gift from the Waseca Chamber of Commerce. David and John planned to collect **pledges** for UNICEF along the way.

The first part of the trip ended in New York. David and John were invited to stay, free of charge, at a Holiday Inn in Manhattan. The manager was surprised when they arrived with a mule. But he found a place for Willie to stay, too.

Making Tracks

David and John never knew what to expect on their trip. In France, the mayor of a village chased them out of his house. In Iran and Turkey, some people threw rocks at them because they were Americans. But most of the people they met were friendly. In Monaco, they were even greeted by Princess Grace.

After John was killed, David flew home. He spent three months **mourning** for his brother and **recuperating** from his wound. But he never thought of giving up his goal of walking around the world. Another brother, Peter, returned with him to the spot where David and John had been attacked. This time the Afghan government provided guards to make sure the Kunst brothers were not harmed.

David and Peter kept walking. Finally, they reached the border of China. There they had to change their route. The Chinese government wouldn't allow them to walk through China. Instead, David and Peter went through India and sailed on to Australia. From there, Peter left David and returned home. David continued his journey alone.

Home at Last

In October of 1974, David walked into Waseca and stepped into the cement footprints he had made four long years before. Peter and Willie Make-It **accompanied** him on the last ten miles of his journey. "Two Kunst brothers began this trip," said Peter, "and two Kunst brothers are going to finish it."

David Kunst walked over 15,000 miles. He crossed four **continents** and 13 countries. He wore out 22 pairs of shoes. David endured both heat and cold to realize his goal. "After walking for four years," said David, "I'll never take things like **air conditioning** and hot showers for granted again. Americans just don't **appreciate** how lucky they are. They probably never will unless they see how some of the rest of the world lives."

David believes that many people would like to have an adventure. They **daydream** about doing something exciting. David hopes that these people will be encouraged by what he has done. "Anyone can do it," he says. "If you make up your mind to do something, you can do it."

Remembering Facts

Read each sentence below. Write **T** if the sentence is true. Write **F** if the sentence is false.

_____ 1. David Kunst used to work as a projectionist at a theater.

_____ 2. David started his walk with his brother and a mule.

_____ 3. The first part of David and John's trip ended in Waseca.

_____ 4. Most of the people the Kunsts met on their trip were friendly.

_____ 5. David and John were both safe after the attack in Afghanistan.

_____ 6. David spent three months recuperating from his wound.

_____ 7. After mourning for his brother, David continued his journey alone.

_____ 8. The Chinese government was very helpful to David and Peter.

_____ 9. David walked back into Waseca in October, 1974.

_____ 10. David walked over 15,000 miles and wore out 22 pairs of shoes.

Finding the Sequence

Write **1** before the sentence that tells what happened first in the story. Write **2** before the sentence that tells what happened next, and so on.

_____ David recorded the first steps of his journey in wet cement.

_____ David and John were attacked by bandits.

_____ David, Peter, and Willie Make-It walked the last ten miles of the journey.

_____ David worked at a theater.

_____ David, John, and Willie Make-It left Waseca.

Using Context

Write the correct word in each blank. Choose from the words below. Use each word only once.

| bored | was | adventure | you |
| make | dream | walk | will |

Many people _____(1)_____ about doing something exciting. David Kunst _____(2)_____ one of these people. He was _____(3)_____. He wanted an _____(4)_____ in his life. So he decided to _____(5)_____ around the world! David Kunst hopes that his journey _____(6)_____ encourage people. He says, "If you _____(7)_____ up your mind to do something, _____(8)_____ can do it."

Drawing Conclusions

Finish each sentence by writing the best answer.

1. When David and John arrived in New York, the manager at the Holiday Inn was surprised because _____

2. In Iran and Turkey, some people threw rocks at David and John because _____

3. David and Peter had to change their route and walk through India because _____

4. David says he'll never take things like air conditioning and hot showers for granted because _____

Identifying Facts and Opinions

Write **F** before each statement that is a fact. Write **O** before each statement that is an opinion.

_____ 1. David Kunst walked over 15,000 miles.

_____ 2. David wore out 22 pairs of shoes.

_____ 3. Willie Make-It is a funny name for a mule.

_____ 4. David and John shouldn't have brought a mule to the Holiday Inn.

_____ 5. Princess Grace greeted David and John in Monaco.

_____ 6. David and John planned to collect pledges for UNICEF.

_____ 7. David and John were attacked by bandits in Afghanistan.

_____ 8. David should have quit the journey after his brother died.

_____ 9. The United States is the best country in the world.

_____ 10. David returned to Waseca in October, 1974.

Writing Your Ideas

Write a letter to David Kunst. Ask him four questions about his journey.

Dear David,

_____

_____

_____

_____

_____

_____

Using Vocabulary

Write the correct word in each sentence.

survey crew	recuperate	pledge
air conditioning	continent	accompany
daydream	mourn	appreciate
projectionist		

1. A person who shows movies in a movie theater is a _____.

2. A promise to give money is a _____.

3. To recover your health and strength is to _____.

4. To feel sorrow for someone's death is to _____.

5. A group of people who measure land is called a _____.

6. When you go with a person, you _____ her or him.

7. To recognize the value of something is to _____ it.

8. The process of cooling and cleaning the air is called _____.

9. One of seven large land areas on Earth is called a _____.

10. To imagine yourself doing something pleasant is to _____.

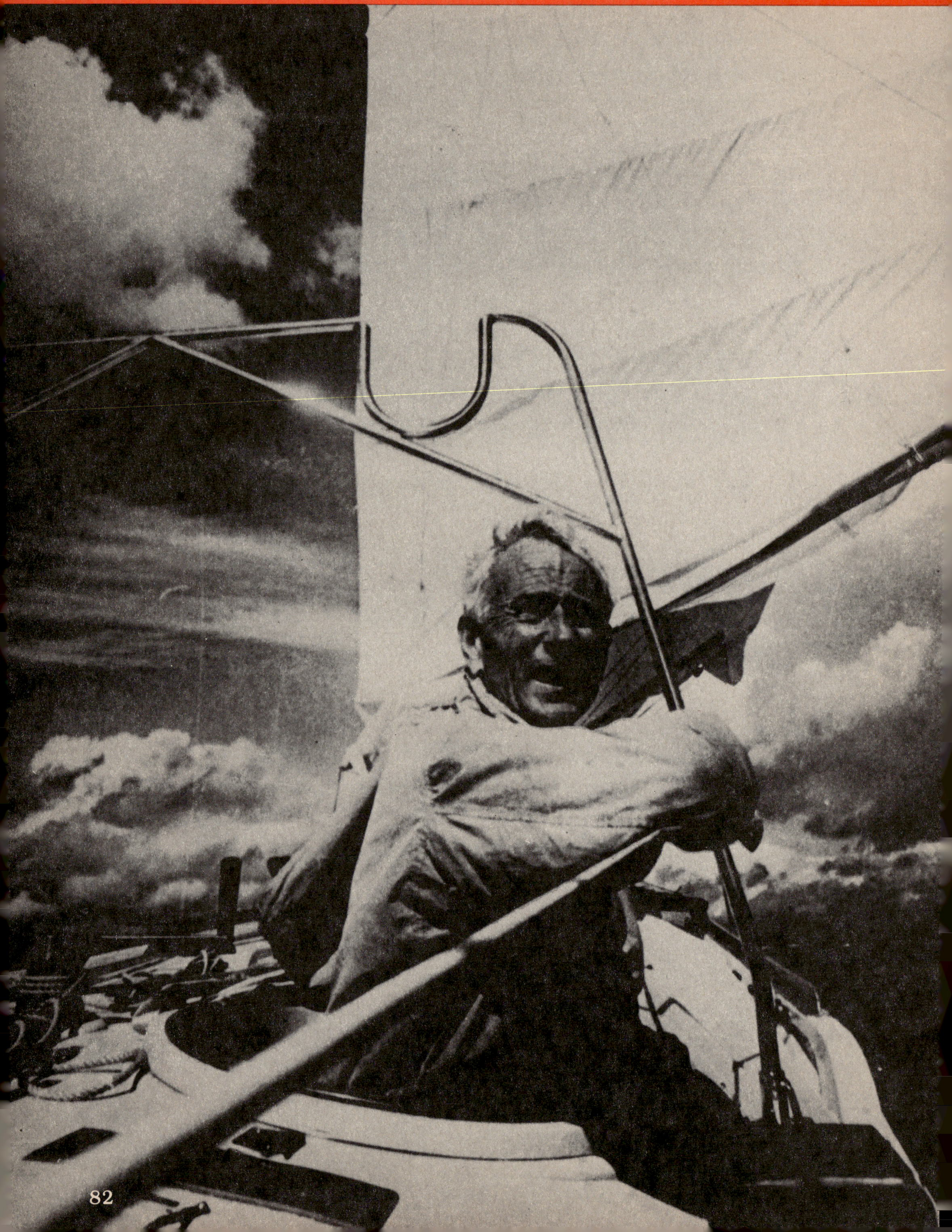

Alone with the Sea

Commander William King was enjoying a perfect day at sea aboard the Galway Blazer II. Suddenly he heard a terrible noise. The hull of the boat gave way before his eyes. Water poured in through a three-foot hole. Commander King rushed to the cockpit to find out what had hit him. He saw a large, dark form swimming away. It was a great white shark! Commander King had to think fast. The Galway Blazer II was sinking.

The Call of the Sea

William King was born in England in 1910. As a boy, he often visited his grandparents on the coast of Scotland. It was there that he fell in love with the sea and learned to sail. He was only 14 years old when he entered the Royal Naval Academy. After he graduated, he became an officer in the British Navy.

During World War II, Bill became a submarine commander. He was the only British submarine commander to survive all six years of combat. His skill and courage made him a hero.

After he retired from the navy, Bill settled down with his wife and children in Oranmore Castle in Galway, Ireland. He enjoyed life in the Irish countryside. He especially loved taking part in the Galway Blazer fox hunt. But after many years, Bill again felt the urge to set sail. "I never felt quite as alive on land as on sea," he said.

The Galway Blazer II

Bill wanted to challenge his sailing **expertise**. So he decided to sail around the world alone by way of Cape Horn. "Cape Horn has a strange **attraction** for sailors," he says. "The Pacific and Atlantic Oceans meet in furiously changing moods. One really can't go anywhere more **violent**. That is part of the challenge, part of the charm."

Bill designed and built a **schooner** for his voyage. It was only 42 feet long. His family was afraid that it would be too small to survive in the open sea. But Bill designed it to be safe. It had a very **buoyant** hull and was **rigged** for easy sailing.

In 1968, Bill set sail from Plymouth Harbor, where he had docked his last submarine after the war. He had plenty of supplies and good books to read. Bill loved the feeling of being alone with the ocean.

Disaster Strikes

The Galway Blazer II was a thousand miles south of Cape Town, South Africa, when disaster struck. Bill was directly in the path of one of the worst

Commander King watches the building of Galway Blazer II.

hurricanes ever to hit that part of the ocean. The Galway Blazer II **weathered** the storm, but capsized in the high waves that followed. The small size of the boat and its rounded lines kept it from being destroyed. The schooner was **intact**, but the mast was snapped off. Bill rigged a **makeshift** mast and managed to reach land. He decided to ship the Galway Blazer II home to be repaired and to spend Christmas with his family.

In the spring of 1969, Bill set out again from Plymouth Harbor. Then, in 1971, the great white shark attacked the schooner and made a hole in the hull. Bill spent ten days pumping water out of his boat and repairing the hole. After 15 desperate days, he reached the coast of Australia. Once again he had to wait for the Galway Blazer II to be repaired.

Bill set out again in 1972. On a stormy, misty February day, he rounded Cape Horn and headed back toward Plymouth Harbor. There he ended his five-year journey. He was met by his family and a large crowd of cheering people. Bill was surprised by their **enthusiasm**. After all, he had only done what he wanted to do.

Remembering Facts

In the blank, write the letter of the best ending for each sentence.

_____ 1. William King was born in
   a. England.   b. Ireland.   c. Scotland.

_____ 2. William entered the Royal Naval Academy at age
   a. 12.   b. 14.   c. 16.

_____ 3. During World War II, Bill became a
   a. submarine commander.   b. fighter pilot.   c. paratrooper.

_____ 4. After he retired from the navy, Bill and his family settled down in
   a. a mobile home.   b. a boat house.   c. Oranmore Castle.

_____ 5. Bill's schooner was
   a. 22 feet long.   b. 42 feet long.   c. 15 feet long.

_____ 6. In 1968, Bill set sail from
   a. Plymouth Harbor.   b. New York Harbor.   c. Boston Harbor.

_____ 7. In 1971, Bill's boat was attacked by a
   a. great white whale.   b. grey dolphin.   c. great white shark.

_____ 8. Bill's journey lasted
   a. one year.   b. ten years.   c. five years.

Finding the Sequence

Write **1** before the sentence that tells what happened first in the story. Write **2** before the sentence that tells what happened next, and so on.

_____ Bill entered the Royal Naval Academy.

_____ Bill designed and built a schooner for his voyage.

_____ Bill rounded Cape Horn and headed back toward Plymouth Harbor.

_____ Bill often visited his grandparents on the coast of Scotland.

_____ Bill became a submarine commander.

Using Context

Write the correct word in each blank. Choose from the words below. Use each word only once.

    than   journey   challenge   feels
    after   decided   around   built

William King says he _____ (1) more alive on sea _____ (2) on land. So, years _____ (3) he retired, he _____ (4) to set sail again. He wanted to take on a _____ (5). He would sail alone _____ (6) the world by way of Cape Horn. Bill designed and _____ (7) a schooner for this voyage. In 1968, he set sail on his _____ (8) in the Galway Blazer II.

Drawing Conclusions

Finish each sentence by writing the best answer.

1. The coast of Scotland had much to do with William King's future because _____

2. Cape Horn has a strange attraction for sailors because _____

3. The Galway Blazer II was not destroyed by the hurricane because _____

4. Bill was surprised by the crowd's enthusiasm on his return because _____

Identifying Facts and Opinions

Write **F** before each statement that is a fact. Write **O** before each statement that is an opinion.

_____ 1. William King was born in 1910.

_____ 2. Bill should have waited until he was older to enter the Royal Naval Academy.

_____ 3. Bill was the only British submarine commander to survive six years of combat in World War II.

_____ 4. Bill's schooner was the safest boat ever built.

_____ 5. It was nice of Bill to spend Christmas with his family.

_____ 6. Bill rounded Cape Horn on a stormy, misty February day.

_____ 7. It was crazy for Bill to continue his voyage after the shark attack.

_____ 8. On his return, Bill was met by a crowd of cheering people.

_____ 9. Nobody should attempt to sail by way of Cape Horn.

_____ 10. Bill's journey lasted five years.

Writing Your Ideas

Pretend you're William King. You're in command of a submarine in World War II. You've been at sea for three months now. Write an entry in your journal telling about your thoughts on this particular day.

_____
_____
_____
_____
_____

Using Vocabulary

Use the clues to complete the puzzle. Choose from the words in the box.

attraction
expertise
enthusiasm
buoyant
violent
schooner
rig
makeshift
weather
intact

Across
3. a strong feeling of excitement
5. fit a ship with masts, sails, lines, etc.
6. a ship with two or more masts
9. not damaged
10. the skill of an expert

Down
1. appeal to desires and tastes
2. substitute
4. able to float
7. has a strong, rough force
8. go through safely

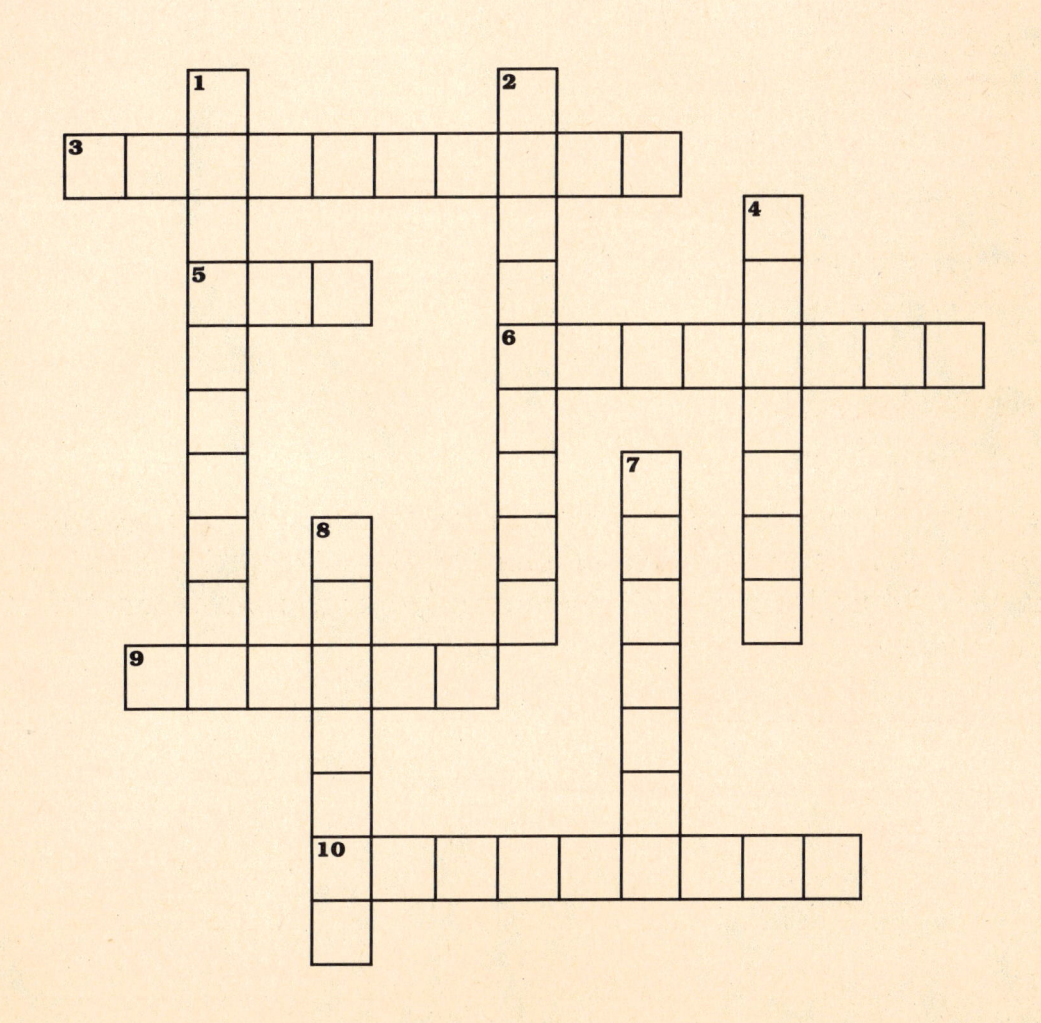

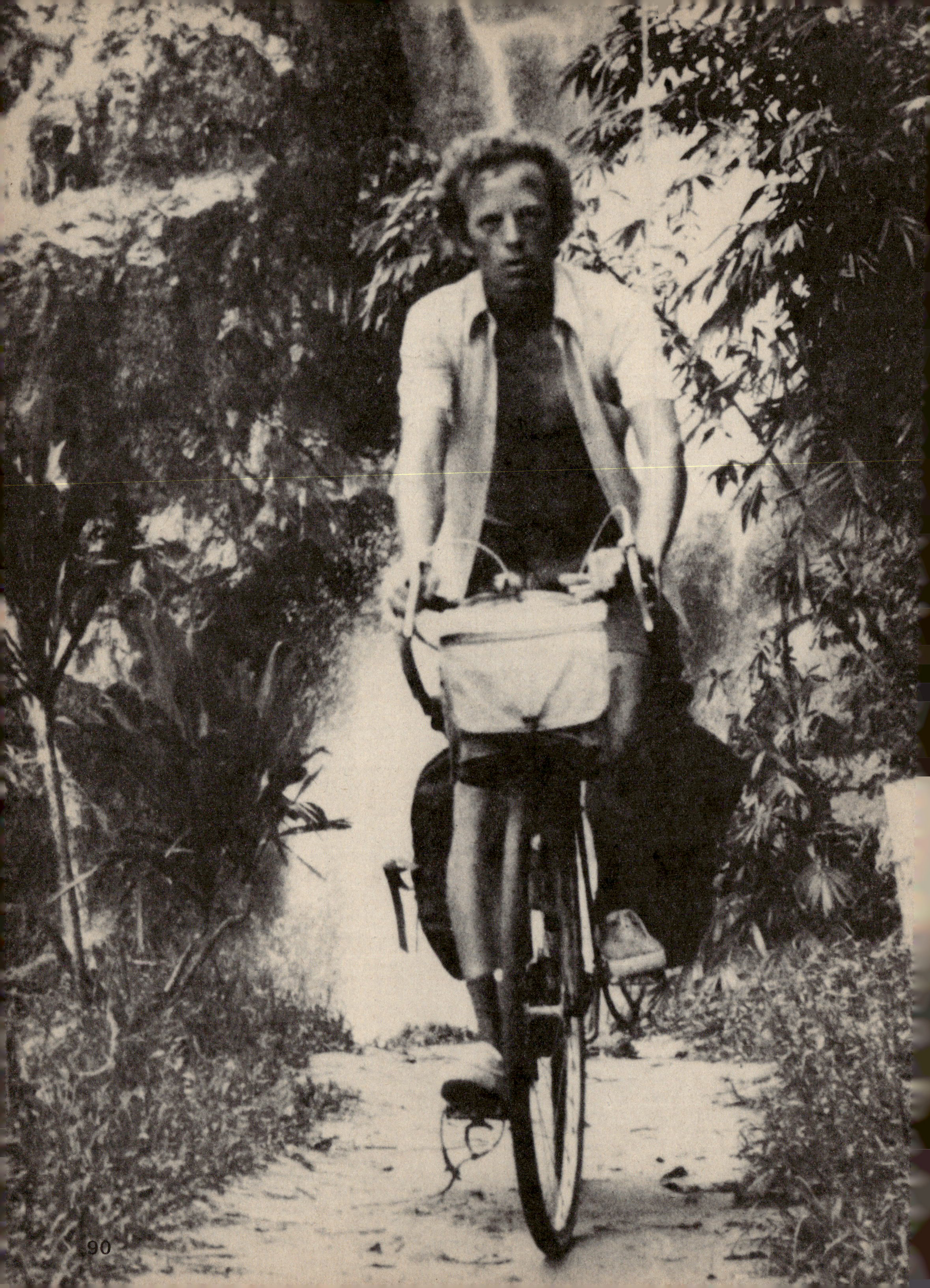

On Two Wheels

Lloyd Sumner was standing in the thick jungle of the Malay **Peninsula**. Suddenly, he heard a noise. "A small **snuffling** sound rose," says Lloyd. "A big bull **boar**, his six-inch **tusks** glistening in the speckled light, charged me. I leaped for a low branch, pulled myself up. The tusks fanned the air just below. Lucky, I told myself, very lucky." Lloyd had made another narrow escape on his journey around the world.

Ready or Not

Lloyd's first job was as an **engineer**. But he wasn't happy with his work. He quit and began creating art on his computer. He made a living by selling his works and giving lectures on computer art. Lloyd had a good life, but it wasn't enough. He wanted to meet a bigger challenge.

Lloyd's friends thought he was crazy. He had little bicycle touring experience. He didn't speak any foreign languages. He wasn't even in good physical shape. But Lloyd Sumner planned to ride his bicycle around the world!

In November of 1971, Lloyd pedaled away from his Virginia home. He had $200 in cash, camping supplies, and two cameras. He also had a brand new bike that he named Maria.

The Road to Adventure

Lloyd began his trip by crossing the United States, including Alaska and Hawaii. Then his route took him over New Zealand and Australia. Next came Sumatra, the Malay Peninsula, Nepal, India, and Africa. Finally, he traveled through Europe. Of course, Lloyd had to cross the oceans by plane or on boats.

Everywhere Lloyd went, people asked him the same questions. They asked him where he was from and where he was going. They wanted to know if he was enjoying his trip. Lloyd made many friends on his journey. He was often invited to stay with people he met. At other times, he stayed in a hotel or even as a guest at the **local** jail.

Not all of the people Lloyd met were friendly. His hat was snatched in Timor. A motorcyclist in Thailand tried to steal the flag off his bike. Children threw rocks at him in Java. And truckers everywhere tried to run him off the road.

Lloyd also had to battle wildlife and the elements. He was **stalked** by a leopard and attacked by a wild boar, a rhinoceros, and an elephant. He endured cold and heat. Once, the patches melted off his bicycle tires because it was so hot. But Lloyd pushed on. He wanted to see the world for himself.

No Regrets

Finally the time came for Lloyd to board a plane back to the United States. He landed in New York and rode his bike back to Virginia, to his own house where he had started almost four years before. He had no regrets.

"I proved a person can accomplish a major goal without outside assistance," says Lloyd. "He can become wealthy by **reducing** his needs rather than by **accumulating** money. I discovered that the purpose of living is to learn as much as possible through experience."

Lloyd Sumner wrote a book about his journey called *The Long Ride*. Now he's ready for a new adventure. He plans to climb the highest point in each state. He also wants to take more trips. "The more I travel," he says, "the more I want to travel. The more I see, the more I realize I haven't seen. It's a **fascinating** world spinning out there, and I, for one, don't want to get off."

Remembering Facts

Read each sentence below. Write **T** if the sentence is true. Write **F** if the sentence is false.

_____ 1. Lloyd Sumner's first job was as an engineer.

_____ 2. Lloyd's friends thought his plan to ride a bike around the world was a great idea.

_____ 3. Maria was the name of Lloyd's girlfriend.

_____ 4. Lloyd began his trip by crossing the United States.

_____ 5. Lloyd made many friends on his journey.

_____ 6. The children in Java were very nice to Lloyd.

_____ 7. Lloyd wrote a book about his journey.

_____ 8. After his bike tour around the world, Lloyd is ready for a quiet life.

_____ 9. Lloyd wants to accumulate a lot of money.

_____ 10. Lloyd has no regrets about what he did.

Finding the Sequence

Write **1** before the sentence that tells what happened first in the story. Write **2** before the sentence that tells what happened next, and so on.

_____ Lloyd boarded a plane back to the United States.

_____ Lloyd quit his job as an engineer.

_____ Lloyd crossed Alaska and Hawaii.

_____ A motorcyclist in Thailand tried to steal the flag off Lloyd's bike.

_____ Lloyd decided to ride his bicycle around the world.

Using Context

Write the correct word in each blank. Choose from the words below. Use each word only once.

    proved   selling   life   challenge
    enough   friends   bike   he

Lloyd Sumner had a good _____(1)_____. He made a living by _____(2)_____ his computer art and giving lectures. But this wasn't _____(3)_____. He wanted a _____(4)_____ in his life. So he decided to ride his _____(5)_____ around the world. His _____(6)_____ thought he was crazy. But _____(7)_____ did it anyway. And he _____(8)_____ that a person doesn't need outside help to accomplish a goal.

Drawing Conclusions

Finish each sentence by writing the best answer.

1. Lloyd quit his job as an engineer because _____

2. Lloyd's friends thought his plan to ride his bike around the world was crazy because _____

3. Once, the patches melted off Lloyd's bicycle because _____

4. Although bad things happened to Lloyd, he pushed on because _____

Identifying Facts and Opinions

Write **F** before each statement that is a fact. Write **O** before each statement that is an opinion.

_____ 1. The people in Thailand are not friendly.

_____ 2. Lloyd started his journey in November, 1971.

_____ 3. Maria is not an appropriate name for a bicycle.

_____ 4. Lloyd crossed the oceans by plane or on boats.

_____ 5. Lloyd was often invited to stay with people he met.

_____ 6. The purpose of life is to accumulate money.

_____ 7. *The Long Ride* is a very interesting book.

_____ 8. At times, Lloyd stayed as a guest at local jails.

_____ 9. All the children in Java are mean.

_____ 10. Lloyd was once attacked by a wild boar.

Writing Your Ideas

Imagine yourself in the middle of the jungle. You have just realized you're being stalked by a leopard. What are you going to do? Write down the first three ideas that come to mind.

1. _____

2. _____

3. _____

Using Vocabulary

Use each of the following words in a sentence. Show by your sentence that you understand the meaning of the word. If you need help, use the Glossary.

1. peninsula

2. snuffling

3. boar

4. tusk

5. engineer

6. local

7. stalk

8. reduce

9. accumulate

10. fascinating

GLOSSARY

accelerator, page 13
The accelerator is the pedal that controls the speed of a car.

accompany, page 77
When you accompany somebody, you go with this person.

accomplish, page 52
When you accomplish something, you get it done.

accumulate, page 93
To accumulate means to collect, little by little.

ace pilot, page 28
An ace pilot is a combat pilot who has brought down at least five enemy airplanes.

air conditioning, page 77
Air conditioning is the process of cooling and cleaning the air.

amateur, page 20
An amateur is a person who is in a sport for fun rather than for money.

amputate, page 68
To amputate is to cut a limb from the body.

appoint, page 29
To appoint a person is to officially name this person for a job.

appreciate, page 77
To appreciate means to recognize the value of something. For example, everyone appreciates a loyal friendship.

approve, page 45
To approve is to give permission.

athlete, page 52
An athlete is a person who is good at and trained in exercises or sports that require skill, strength, and speed.

attitude, page 44
Your attitude is your way of acting, feeling, and thinking.

attraction, page 84
Something that has attraction draws people by appealing to their desires and tastes.

avalanche, page 60
An avalanche is a large mass of snow and ice that comes down a mountainside with great speed.

aviation, page 5
Aviation means air travel.

ballast, page 20
Ballast is something heavy, like bags of sand, that is placed in the gondola of a balloon to control the altitude. It also helps keep the balloon stable.

balloonist, page 20
A balloonist is a person whose sport is traveling in a balloon.

benefit (noun), page 37
A benefit is something that helps a person or thing.

benefit (verb), page 44
When you benefit from something, you gain something valuable.

boar, page 91
A boar is a wild pig.

boarding school, page 36
A boarding school is a school where students can live and eat all their meals.

bravery, page 19
Bravery means courage.

buoyant, page 84
Something that is buoyant is able to float.

capsize, page 67
To capsize means to turn upside down.

cockpit, page 4
The cockpit is the place in an airplane where the pilot sits.

collapse, page 68
To collapse is to fall down suddenly.

combat, page 28
Combat is active fighting in a war.

competitively, page 12
When you do something competitively, your goal is to win.

continent, page 77
A continent is one of seven large land areas on Earth. The continents are Asia, Africa, North America, South America, Antarctica, Europe, and Australia.

craft, page 68
A craft is a small boat.

crisis, page 29
A crisis is a difficult or dangerous situation in which a decision has to be made.

current, page 45
A current is a strong flow of water that moves along in a path.

daydream, page 77
When you daydream, you imagine yourself doing something pleasant or doing something you've always wanted to do.

depressed, page 68
When you are depressed, you feel very sad and gloomy.

determined, page 37
If you are a determined person, you know what you want and work to accomplish it.

diary, page 61
A diary is a written record of the things one does each day.

dietetics, page 36
Dietetics is the science that deals with the amount and kind of food needed by the body.

disability, page 52
A disability is a lack of ability. For example, Rick Hansen has a physical disability. He lacks the ability to walk.

dolphin, page 43
A dolphin is a very intelligent sea animal that is related to the whale. It has a snout that is like a beak and two flippers.

donation, page 53
A donation is a gift. For example, Rick Hansen had enough money to continue his trip because of the donations people gave him.

downdraft, page 20
A downdraft is a downward movement of air.

elements, page 44
The elements are the forces of nature such as rain, wind, and snow.

elevation, page 60
Elevation is the height above the surface of Earth.

encourage, page 37
When you encourage someone, you give him or her hope, confidence, and courage.

endurance, page 4
Endurance is the ability to keep on going when under hardship, stress, etc.

engineer, page 92
An engineer is a person trained to plan the building of bridges, roads, machines, etc.

enthusiasm, page 85
Enthusiasm is a strong feeling of excitement and interest about something.

expedition, page 60
An expedition is a journey that has a special purpose. For example, the purpose of the Hunt expedition was to climb Mount Everest.

experimental, page 4
Something that is experimental is something that is being tested or tried out.

expertise, page 84
Expertise is the skill of an expert.

exposure, page 20
Exposure is the condition of being exposed without protection to the effects of severe weather.

extreme, page 44
Extreme means very great or severe.

fascinating, page 93
Something that is fascinating is extremely interesting.

flexible, page 4
Something that is flexible is not stiff and can bend without breaking.

frigid, page 44
Frigid means extremely cold.

generate, page 45
To generate means to produce or bring about. For example, Lynne Cox had to swim as fast as she could to stay warm. Her fast movements generated heat.

gondola, page 20
The gondola is the passenger compartment that hangs beneath a balloon.

gusty, page 60
Wind that has sudden rushes of air is called gusty.

hang glider, page 20
A hang glider is a glider that looks like a kite. A harnessed rider hangs from it while gliding down from a high place.

horsepower, page 11
Horsepower is a unit for measuring the power of an engine.

hull, page 69
The sides and bottom of a boat or ship are called the hull.

impulse, page 12
When you do something on impulse, you do it suddenly and without giving it much thought.

individual, page 19
Something individual has to do with one person. An individual act is an act done by one person.

instructor, page 12
An instructor is a teacher.

intact, page 85
Something that remains intact has not been damaged in any way. For example, the Galway Blazer II remained intact after the terrible storm.

invest, page 4
To invest means to give or spend time, effort, or money in hopes of reaching a goal.

knighted, page 61
When a man is knighted, he is honored for doing a service to his country. This man becomes a knight and uses the word "Sir" before his name.

local, page 92
Something that is local has to do with a particular place. For example, a local park is one near you.

Mach 1, page 27
Mach 1 is the speed of sound.

magnificent, page 21
Something that is magnificent is strikingly beautiful or grand. For example, if you ride in a balloon, you get a magnificent view of the world below.

makeshift, page 85
Something that is makeshift is a substitute for the correct thing.

marathon, page 52
A marathon is a long-distance race.

mission, page 27
When you are sent on a mission, you are given a special task to do.

mourn, page 76
To mourn is to feel and express sorrow for someone's death.

myth, page 69
A myth is a legend about the heroes or ancestors of a group of people.

natural, page 13
Being a natural at something means that you are born with the ability to do it well.

occasion, page 45
An occasion is an important or special event.

peninsula, page 91
A peninsula is a portion of land that is almost totally surrounded by water.

pledge, page 76
A pledge is a promise to give money.

porter, page 60
A porter is a person who carries heavy things for other people.

potential, page 52
Having potential means having an ability that may or may not be developed. For example, Rick Hansen wants people with disabilities to see they have the potential to do many things.

predict, page 36
To predict is to tell in advance.

projectionist, page 76
A projectionist is a person who shows movies in a movie theater.

rank, page 28
A rank is an official position in the armed forces.

recruiter, page 28
A recruiter is a person in charge of enlisting new soldiers for the army, navy, etc.

recuperate, page 76
When you recuperate, you recover your health and strength after an illness or accident.

reduce, page 93
When you reduce something, you make it smaller in size, amount, or number.

refuel, page 4
To refuel means to take on additional fuel.

respond, page 12
To respond is to answer.

responsibility, page 37
When you take on responsibility, you make your own choices about important matters.

rig, page 84
To rig a ship means to fit it with masts, sails, lines, etc.

schooner, page 84
A schooner is a ship that has two or more masts.

scuba, page 12
Scuba (Self-Contained Underwater Breathing Apparatus) is the equipment used for breathing while swimming underwater.

severe, page 69
Severe means violent and very harsh.

smuggler, page 69
A smuggler is a person who takes things in and out of a country secretly and against the law.

snuffling, page 91
A snuffling sound is the sound made by breathing through the nose like a person with a head cold.

sound barrier, page 29
When a plane breaks the sound barrier, it flies faster than the speed of sound.

speedometer, page 27
The speedometer is the instrument that shows how fast a vehicle is moving.

stalk, page 92
To stalk means to follow quietly and carefully. For example, Lloyd Sumner was stalked by a leopard.

suicide, page 53
Suicide is the act of killing oneself.

summit, page 60
Summit means highest point. The summit of a mountain is the highest point of that mountain.

survey crew, page 76
A survey crew is a group of people who measure land to find out its size, shape, and boundaries.

survive, page 5
To survive is to stay alive.

terrain, page 60
Terrain is another word for ground.

trimaran, page 67
A trimaran is a fast sailboat that has three hulls side by side.

turbulence, page 4
Turbulence is a disturbance caused by up-and-down movements of air.

tusk, page 91
A tusk is a long, pointed tooth that sticks out of the side of the mouth of certain animals.

typhoon, page 5
A typhoon is the name given to hurricanes in the western Pacific Ocean area.

unexpected, page 36
Something unexpected is something that happens without warning.

unique, page 36
Unique means very unusual or uncommon. For example, Hulda Crooks has a unique old age because she does things other people her own age would never consider doing.

vegetarian, page 36
A vegetarian diet is a diet consisting mainly of vegetables.

veteran, page 60
A veteran is a person with much experience. For example, John Hunt was a veteran mountain climber.

vibration, page 12
A vibration is a quivering or trembling motion.

violent, page 84
Something that is violent has a strong, rough force.

water-skiing, page 12
Water-skiing is the sport of skiing on the water.

weather, page 85
To weather a storm means to go through it safely.

wheelchair, page 50
A wheelchair is a chair that is mounted on wheels. Wheelchairs are used by people who cannot walk.